HAULING HEAVYWEIGHTS

The techniques of heavy haulage explained.

HAULING
HEAVYWEIGHTS
Moving Extra-large Loads by Road

Bob Tuck

Patrick Stephens, Wellingborough

First published in 1986

British Library Cataloguing in Publication Data

Tuck, Bob
    Hauling heavyweights—moving extra-large
    loads by road
    1. Commercial vehicles—Geat Britain
    —History
    I. Title
    629.2'24'0941   TL230
    ISBN 0-85059-827-3

*Patrick Stephens Limited is part of the
Thorsons Publishing Group*

Printed and bound in Great Britain.

Contents

Introduction

Describe it coldly and heavy haulage is not that exciting. Pick something up, move it, then put it down is a perfectly correct interpretation, but how is it done, how do you move an object of 10, 100 or even 1,000 tons in weight? In these days of load-carrying trailers with so many wheels they just seem uncountable, we just take it for granted. Teams of powerful tractors have physically pushed and pulled three and four thousand tons which seems to make a mockery of the days of old when anything of 10 to 15 tons was really quite a heavy load. Modern-day mobile cranes can lift 500 to 600 tons with boring ease when less than a century ago it was a major achievement just to lift a large tree trunk on to the back of a horse and cart.

My fourth book on the subject of road-going heavy haulage, *Hauling Heavyweights* reflects the strides that man has made both with his equipment and his technique in this field of transportation. The photographs have been taken from sources throughout the country, while the stories are from men who regularly demonstrate that whilst the difficult job is done every day, the downright impossible may take just slightly longer.

Acknowledgements

I would like to thank all who have assisted with this book either in the furnishing of photographs or in help with research. I would specifically like to mention the following companies: BNFL; Distington Engineering; Dow Mac (Concrete Products) Ltd; ICI; ITM; Evesham Journal; Middlesbrough Evening Gazette; NEI. The following people have also been of great assistance: Dave Abbott; John Banks; Peter Clemmett; Paul Hancox; Jack Higgins; Jack Hill; Alan Martin; John Marshall; Chris Miller; George Nairn; Howard Nunnick; Arthur Philipson; Norman Reed; Tim Wayne; David Silbermann; Peter Sunter; Maurice Webb and Rick and Dennis. It would be remiss of me not to mention Sylvia who continues to be a source of both guidance and inspiration.

Bob Tuck
Yarm, January 1986

Chapter 1

The ground rules are set

Undoubtedly the road has been with us in one form or another since time immemorial but as far as heavy haulage is concerned, it was the coming of the railway that demonstrated the way ahead. The railmen however had the benefit of a specially laid down track with bends eliminated to a gentle curve and gradients eased to a minimum, whilst the road haulier simply inherited what was made by his fore-fathers with perhaps the toiling oxen the heaviest thing it was ever planned to bear. The Romans proved to be incredible road makers, their philosophy of building straight and true still forming the pattern of many of our modern day highways although with a degree of mixed blessings. The A1 through North Yorkshire follows the Roman path of Dere Street and its line and direction can only seek praise. Further north in Durham however that same straight Dere Street has an ominous reputation when it forms the Chair Bank at Ebchester, one of the steepest inclines in the area, as it descends dramatically to cross the River Derwent. The bridges of the railmen were freshly built with iron and steel, the epitome of strength. The counterparts on the roads were ancient and weathered stone structures, slowly eroding through neglect so it is no wonder that, all things considered, when it came to moving really concentrated weights the railways had it made.

The road-going heavy haulier was a confused man. His horse and cart was definitely not up to such tasks, no matter how much it was 'beefed up' so it was only natural that he endeavoured to copy the equipment used by the railways. This was not always successful however—steel wheels may be all right when they run on a steel road-way but place that same heavily-loaded wheel on to roadstone or tarmacadam and it will simply sink. The steel roadwheels were made fatter and then coated in rubber to spread this weight but neverthe-less a necessary and over-used part of equipment on the road train's

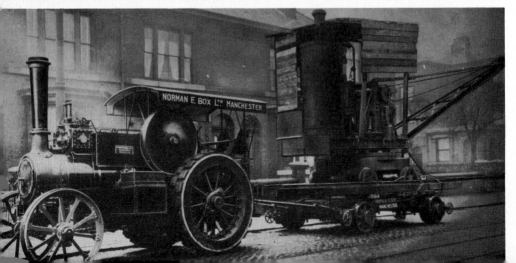

Left *The early road-going equipment was rather crude in its construction, this trailer of Wakefield-based Spur Inmans offered very little in the way of suspension or steering. The Fowler Class B6 compound locomotive No 12226 was registered number HL 930, it was new in 1911.*

Below left *Norman E. Box bought this compound McLaren locomotive No 1570 known as* Rover *new in 1918. It was fitted with Boulton spring wood block segmented rear wheels. Carrying the 20-ton Booth steam crane, this Fowler trailer offered no form of steering turntable, this being replaced by two detachable drawbars. Cornering was performed by detaching one of the bars and dragging the trailer round on its axis. The load carrier is seen to be fitted with four hand wheels which were used to wind on the individual wooden brake blocks.*

Above and below *Even with making the road wheels wider it still meant the weight was concentrated on to four very small points. Any slight weakness in the road surface could be picked out although these shots of Harper & Screen's Burrell having lost its load due to a drain collapse did not reflect a regular occurrence. Harper & Screen were the predecessors of Screen Bros of Oldbury, Birmingham who were prominent in heavy haulage in the Midlands during the 1920s and '30s.*

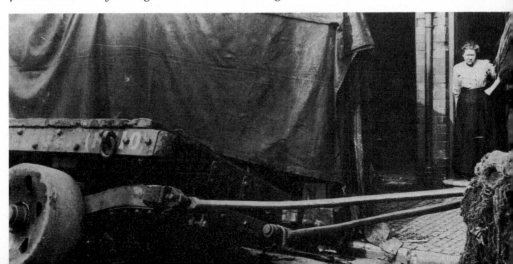

tackle wagon were steel plates to lay down over soft stretches of road.
An early pioneer, Norman E. Box, was one of the first to realize that if
these plates were made in a round shape then they could be simply
bowled forward on their edge by one man for reuse rather than
requiring two or more men to handle a similar-sized square or rec-
tangular plate.

Even at the beginning of the twentieth century heavy road haulage
was a hard and demanding profession but one thing the railway
companies could rarely offer was a total transportation package. It is
true that railway lines could be and were built in and out of factories,
steel plants and shipyards. On occasion you could load your casting
or boiler on to the rail truck at your factory and have it delivered to
your customer never having left that steel track. But often railway
lines proved too unadaptable—financial and practical constraints
meant that railways couldn't go everywhere. It was this area of adapt-
ability where road transport left the railways standing. It could carry
things into the deepest forests or up some of the steepest hills, it
didn't really matter if there was an official road there or not, the road-
going heavy haulier simply improvised his way round things.

The railways had their own physical problems like the restrictions
imposed by narrow tunnels, low bridges and closely adjacent oppos-
ing track but what rankled the big railway companies most was that
the road men were mainly independent operators determined to
make a living by their own ingenuity and had no form of direct control
over them as a group. The political muscle that the railway companies
were able to exert is reflected in the laws that were created in the early
1930s which, in modified form, still apply to road transport operations today. Whilst there is virtually no limit to the length and weight
of British Rail's coal trains, in the mid-1980s the road-going operator
generally must not exceed 60 ft and he cannot carry any more than 20
or 25 tons of payload.

The heavy haulier, however, knew that his business of moving the
outsize, outweight loads could never be done completely by the railways so an uneasy truce was drawn between the two parties for with
many cross-country loads they were obliged to work very closely
together. One particular company who formed a very good liaison
with the railway operators was Bentleys of Bradford. They acquired a
very good reputation for moving and installing anything heavy or
awkward, with a lot of their traffic being either from or to the adjacent
railheads. Limited craneage of perhaps 15 or 20 tons capacity was
sometimes available at some of the go-ahead stations for transshipp-

ing smaller loads, but for anything with real weight the heavy hauliers were obliged to improvise and devise a method to skid the load sidewards, from rail to road vehicle. The steam road locomotives with spinning fly wheel and power on tap were nearly always found with a winch as part of their basic equipment which was normally concealed inside one of the rear wheel hubs. Disengaging the road-wheel drive allowed the power to be applied to the rotating winch drum. Moving anything sideways is always easier than trying to lift against the force of gravity and to ease friction either greased plates, small rollers—doddlers as they were known—or in the case of Bentley, steel cricket-type balls were used in channels so that after jacking up, transhipping was simply a matter of hauling sideways. The railways were certainly quicker across the ground than their road-going counterparts but transfers like this from road to rail then back again

Bradford railway station was quite a go-ahead place in that it offered the facilities of a 20-ton capacity overhead crane, thus unloading this 11-ft high, 19-ton 2,500-KVA transformer during March 1926 prior to the road haul to Thornbury sub-station was a fairly easy job for the Bentley staff. The locomotive is a Class B5 compound Fowler No 9495, registered AK 9024, of 1904 vintage.

Above and below *The technique of side winching was the more normal method of transferring heavy weights from rail to road load carrier, or vice versa. This Parsons alternator stator is destined for Derby Corporation Electricity works at Full Street, Derby and weighed in at 45 tons. It was railed to Derby London and North Eastern Railway station on 24 September 1929. Particularly interesting are the steel cricket-like balls that Bentley utilized to roll the load sideways.*

Seen about 1925, London Traction's Class R3 compound Fowler No 12749, which carried its own limited craneage, is transhipping this 63-ton stator destined for Hackney. The trailer is a substantial 50-ton Fowler unit with wind-on hand brakes to the rear wheels, but it still has a very much railway look about its design.

were time consuming and strenuous exercises. Attempts were made to use trailers that could be hauled both by road and rail but these load carriers never proved practical, and it soon became more economic, for short hauls at least, to do the whole journey by road. Equally when anything excessively big or wide was involved the road men could always prove their worth.

The archives of Pickfords show that in January 1938 they moved what was reported to be the world's biggest bulk load. A Ruth's steam accumulator measuring 70 ft long, 12 ft diameter and weighing 90 tons was road hauled 325 miles from Annan, Dumfriesshire to the Gas and Light Coke Co's Beckton gas works in Essex. Eighteen months' preparation had preceded this massive move but when the three Fowler engines, *Atlas, Talisman* and *Jix* set off north from their base at Manchester to pick the load up, they could not get over Shap due to deep snow. One thing that heavy hauliers do is always give in to weather conditions like this, although the men weren't too upset as it meant they could spend Christmas and New Year at home. Three weeks later the trio repeated their steps north but it still took three

Above and below *The concept of carrying your load slung between two parallel horizontals goes back to the beginning of time but these two photographs illustrate the similarity of both rail and road trains using this method of transport. Begrudgingly, one has to admit that the railway shot taken in May 1948 looks a far better set as it is seen about to leave for Bristol. The Rudd's Scammells are hauling a transformer destined for Croydon in July 1950 which is resting on bogies also of Scammell manufacture.*

Above and below *The heavy-hauling low loaders also bore a very close resemblance to London and North Eastern Railway's six-axled vehicle (above) which was able to carry either 81 tons when supported over the bogies or 70 tons in the central position. It is about to leave for Northampton in May 1940. The Norman E. Box Fowler trailer of similar line (below) offered an 85-ton capacity on four axles. It is seen about to leave Heaton for a short run to Birtley with a 64-ton 15,000-KVA transformer on 20 March 1936.*

days to clear Shap, the snow at the time being 9 in deep. The haul
itself was completed without incident, the eighteen travelling days
bringing an average road speed of about 2 mph. The records show
that the Fowlers consumed approximately 20 tons of coal for the journey between them, water being evaporated by the trio at the rate of
3,000 gallons per day.

The mighty road-going steamers were certainly an impressive sight
but like a highly-strung thoroughbred they could be fidgety and quite
a handful. Their working principle of producing power through
steam was virtually identical to that of the railway locomotive and
some of the equipment used was also based on railway rolling stock
which could prove a serious problem, for example some trailers were
not even steerable so sheer brute force was required to change direction. These load carriers were regularly fitted with drawbars that
could be split in half. Performing a turn involved one half of the

One method of rail carriage that road men could not fully emulate is shown by this
stator bound for Keadby in Lincolnshire. The use of cantilevers working through a
set of fulcrums promotes an ability to spread the weight down more supporting axles.

Above and below *On 8 March 1950 J. W. Kitchenham recorded E. W. Rudd's old fleet flagship, their R100-based AJD 140, finishing the end of a long rail haul from Newcastle to Bournemouth. The Parsons stator is carried through the bore so that its railway running height is kept to a minimum. The frame trailer is a home-made Rudd special, their solid-tyred bogies being of Scammell manufacture.*

Above and below *The Liverpool trailer manufacture of Dyson always prided themselves in being one of the forerunners of innovation. However this three-axle, 75-ton capacity unit new to Road Engines and Kerr in 1937 still looks rather dated in its concept. It is pictured (above) in November 1943 loaded with a 59-ton gear case bound for the Caledon Shipbuilding Company of Dundee headed up by Burrell engine* Clyde *registration number GA 7818. One thing the trailer withstood was the passage of time for it is also seen (below) headed up by Pickfords Birtley-based MLC 810 hauling a 68-ton stator bound for Dublin in about 1957.*

Installation was all part and parcel of the heavy-haulage profession but lowering this 26-ton transformer to the ground in Forth Brown's works at Sheffield in May 1934 probably took three or four days to complete. One end of the birdcage, as it was known, would be jacked at a time allowing timbers to be removed at the other side. This slow, laborious process has been replaced nowadays by highly efficient mobile craneage.

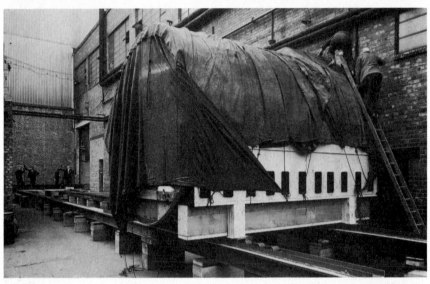

drawbar being disconnected and the trailer pulled round on its axis to point in the required direction. Putting steel plates down on the road eased the friction and sometimes the fire brigade were asked to hose the granite cobbles to make the manoeuvre less painful. I suppose it was an effective idea but it was excruciatingly slow and harsh both on the wheels and on the roadway. The technology available to the heavy haulier seemed very slow or very expensive in the developing of suitable equipment although his technique seemed unboundable.

Raising something from ground level could be extremely difficult in the days when power jacks were not even a day dream. A story is told however of one particular awkward load that Bentleys were asked to move with not even a glimpse of daylight between it and the ground. The enterprising solution adopted by the Yorkshiremen was to simply dig a hole adjacent to the load and pull the trailer in so that it was in close proximity to the load. This charge was then simply dragged sideways on to the trailer bed and with the load carrier winched back out of the hole it was business as usual with yet another problem surmounted.

Some of the big names in road-going heavy haulage built up quite a reputation for themselves with tricks like this, although it was perhaps in the heart of our deepest forests that they were tested to the limit. There were no such things as overhead cranes in these places and even a substantial road was quite a luxury. What forest work did was to make the haulier think: how do you pick up a massive tree trunk when you have just felled it to the ground; how do you place it on the back of the vehicle; what sort of vehicle do you use to move these trees when they could be anything up to 80 ft long?

The timber haulier was obliged to master the laws of physics in order to use his limited horse power to its maximum effect. If his rope couldn't take the strain he would put it through a series of pulley blocks to multiply its capacity. Crude ramping was used to rotate trees up on to the back of the carrying vehicle whilst the principle of lashing three legs together to form a substantial tripod was one method regularly used if a direct upward lifting point was needed.

Left *One technique not really superseded by cranes is this method of movment and although the photographs were taken on 15 May 1964 they are of a timeless nature. The manual monkey winches are still in current use when it is not practical to utilize power winching. The brand new packing standing about 20 in high marries up with the unloading height of the 90-ton capacity Crane four-axle girder trailer. It would have taken a full day to travel from the trailer to the end of the alley way.*

Above *London Traction Haulage Co was taken over by Pickfords about 1930. Their Fowler road locomotive number 14115, The Lion of 1914, registration XC 9653, is seen hauling a Ruston steam navvy with a tackle trailer coupled on behind. Even in the early pioneering days this seems a questionable technique, and was probably for a short move only, or it may even have been posed specially for the camera. The Fowler was passed on again to Walter Denton and is reportedly still in existence in the Southport area.*

Below *The Wynn family had strong interests in timber haulage. Two of their 4 × 4 Unipowers, built by Universal Power Drive of Perivale, Middlesex, are on show in the Welshpool area during the late 1940s. JAE 95 was bought from the Forestry Commission whilst Hannibal LME 89 started life in 1939 as a demonstrator and was bought by Wynn's in 1944. The vehicle in the centre is a Caterpillar D4 crawler tractor.*

Tom Sunter was not a pioneer in the timber field but the solution that he adopted in devising a suitable vehicle to haul these lengthy loads was an example of how road-going heavy haulage was to eventually break away from its railway influence.

The Sunter Brothers had been in the light haulage business for just under ten years and they found excessive competition creeping into the cattle-carrying trade in which they were engaged. Looking elsewhere for customers, Tom Sunter settled on the timber trade of North Yorkshire. The mixed fleet of platform vehicles could readily cope with finished products like pit props, but what the customers, like Hird and Gibson of Marske, really wanted was for vehicles to haul trees straight from the forest direct to the new mills. An artic was the obvious answer but there wasn't one in the fleet so they just got down and made one. People like Scammell had been producing their articulated six-wheelers for some time so the concept wasn't new although the technique that the Sunters adopted was certainly different.

A petrol-engined Bedford was first stripped of its beast-carrying body and after the bowed chassis was levelled out with shaped timbers, a steel plate was positioned across the centre of the chassis frame. The crude fifth wheel was in the form of a baulk of timber laid on the steel plate. A hole was drilled through the baulk, the plate with a locating pin being placed through this hole and all was held in position by a cotter pin underneath the steel plate.

Coupled to this sophisticated tractor was a very basic semi-trailer, well telegraph poles must be considered fairly basic! The base of the pole was bolted on to the timber fifth wheel baulk by L-shaped brackets. The running gear took the form of an old Dennis chassis cut down to leave the rear axle assembly only. The telegraph pole was simply laid over this chassis and held loosely in position by two bands running over the top of the pole from the chassis cross members. The idea of this being loose was so that the axle could be moved backwards and forwards along the pole to accommodate the differing lengths of tree to be hauled. Once in position a chain was wrapped round the pole and chassis then twisted tight by using a small sapling or anything handy. This in turn was roped tight to the telegraph pole and with the fitting of bolsters front and rear, the slick-operating trombone artic was ready for the road.

Leonard Sunter took the wheel for the first load of trees to Wickersley, Rotherham, with John Robinson acting as mate, and things didn't start off very well. By 10 pm on the first day they had

Left *The present Chris Miller can date his origins in haulage back to 1837, although it was his grandfather who really built the company up in the early 1900s. They too were very much involved in the timber trade (as shown in the photograph top) and utilizing tricks learned in the forest they were able to pick up a 40-ft long, 16-ft wide, 14-ft high office suite using sets of three legs. The haul was done in 1925 without a pane of glass being broken as shown middle. The small transformer shown bottom was being moved from Preston docks to the Ribble Power Station in August 1928.*

Above *In February 1942 E. W. Rudd moved this 112-ton stator destined for Melbourne, Australia. They carried it through the bore, railway fashion, the weight being taken on their eight-wheel Scammell bogies. The pushing tractor was R. T. & J. Hewitt's Morpeth-based steam Sentinel No 9260, registration JR 5342, which was new in 1936.*

only managed to get from Great Ayton to Thirsk and had suffered two punctures en route. A foot of snow fell that night so the journey down to South Yorkshire had more than its share of drama but the load was safely delivered.

This was the start of the movement of many trees, some up to 90 ft in length. Although things were rarely as exciting as the first run, there was still the odd moment. John Robinson was driving one day and got caught for exceeding the 20 mph speed limit near Aberford. Not only that but he was told by the law that he couldn't drive artics as he was two years short of being the required 21 years old. This was easily rectified as Len took over the driving but it was only half an hour later when they realized he should not be driving either as he did not have a current driving licence.

An increase in custom meant a single driver operating the artic. Normally this was all right until it came to working the trailer brake.

This was cable operated with a wire running down the pole from the trailer axle into the cab. It had to be kept slack to allow for the ever bending articulation in the vehicle, so when the brake had to be applied a small hand wheel was operated to tighten the cable. In theory this was fine but in practice you were miles past the place you were braking for by the time you had wound the wheel, making the entire operation superfluous. A more practical part of the artic was that the pole semi-trailer was made of wood. Whenever it broke, which was a regular occurrence, a visit to the forest saw a suitable tree selected, sawn down and substituted for the broken one, putting business back to normal.

The first artic operated by the Sunter brothers was certainly crude, but could this simple concept really change the style of heavy haulage?

Chapter 2

Ballasted tractor or articulated combination

Changing one's way of thought can sometimes be very difficult, especially if it is deeply entrenched. The configuration of a large locomotive pulling an independent trailer by means of a drawbar had been established as the only real heavy haulage machine since mechanized movement started. Anyway the artic was just a new-fangled idea of getting round the speed and weight limits imposed on vehicles drawing a trailer, it could never be used for heavy haulage could it?

Scammell had amongst their staff men who must not have agreed with that line of thought, for out of their Watford works came some of the first articulated low loaders to take to the road. The smooth shape of the front of the trailer as it tapered down to the carrying area coined the term 'swan neck' which is still in use today. In fact the con-figuration of those early low loaders with four wheels in line at the rear of the semi-trailer predominated on this type of vehicle for nearly fifty years and they can still be seen in use today. These four wheels were cheekily termed as forming two axles with two wheels on each axle and in the main were made to be removable (for loading/unloading purposes), being termed as knock-out axles. In theory it was a simple matter of jacking the rear of the trailer up at either side and then, after removing any locking pins, to simply slide the two pairs of wheels off and bowl them away. In practice this procedure varied from being difficult to almost impossible. Up to 11 tons a wheel could be legally carried on each of those wheels thus jacking some-thing like this with mechanical side jacks took a feat of superhuman strength. The locking pins regularly seized up through all the road dirt they were subject to and rarely was the unloading point level, making jacking up even more difficult.

The alternative to the conventional low loader was a half-way version referred to as being a step frame. This allowed fairly small rear

Above *Even for smaller loads the ballasted tractor-drawbar trailer outfit was favoured for some, GX 2396 being Currie's fleet number 222. Used in this form meant a greater flexibility of trailers in the days before more sophisticated fifth-wheel couplings on semi-trailers. The load carried in this photograph from early 1939 is an oil radiator cooler for transformer use.*

Below *The articulated low loaders offered by Scammell were a major step forward in the type of vehicle available to the heavy hauliers. Currie's of Newcastle operated three of these outfits, GK 4321 rated as having a questionable capacity for 50-ton loads. It is pictured in November 1937 with a 25-ton transformer destined for the Metropolitan Electric Supply Company of Southall, Middlesex.*

The configuration of the four-in-line low-loading semi-trailer has remained in use for sixty years although a possibility of blow outs on the large rearmost tyres has meant that any escorting police motor cyclists who follow behind have been kept wide awake! Sunter operated a batch of these popular 11.3-engined Mammoth Majors.

wheels to be mounted underneath the trailer frame itself although these wheels were not normally designed to be removed. One advantage of the step frame was that the loading area could be made longer on a similar length vehicle although loading anything via the rear was aided by tapering the rear of the trailer or giving it a 'beaver tail' as it was called. To the heavy haulier having the loading platform as near to the ground as possible was certainly a boon but getting too top heavy was not really a problem as Howard Nunnick discovered. He was helping plant dealer Foster Willan to collect a 22RB base machine one day but instead of using the old low loader with knock-out axles, they were using a tandem-axle step-frame semi-trailer which was a good foot higher. Howard expressed concern over the centre of gravity but unperturbed Foster simply said that he would pick it up the next day when he came back for the boom and buckets!

These small low loaders soon found general acceptance. The step up to Scammell's mighty twins, their first hundred-tonners, was slightly different and although in the mid-1980s we may take it for granted that artics could carry loads well into three figures worth of weight, in 1929 it hit the industry like a massive bombshell. The fact that there were only two of these monsters built suggests that they

Opposite top *The idea of a semi-low loader or step-frame trailer prompted some strange home-made designs which appeared to have a rather tail-up attitude about them because of conventional running gear. This photograph taken in June 1958 illustrates a Sunter variation, the 40-ft main deck coming originally from an American Fruehauf trailer, whilst EYY 593 was one of a batch of ex-Shell Scammell tractors.*

Opposite middle *Hill of Botley also converted some American equipment into step-frame semi-trailers, the slight reduction in height yet long platform being appreciated when they moved these 15-ft wide sections from Chichester to the Midlands in about 1962. GYF 492 and HGT 452, two ex-Shell Scammells are pictured northbound on the A33 at Spitfire bridge.*

Opposite bottom and below *Wynn's built semi-trailer 331 with inlaid lines especially for the carriage of railway equipment. The BTH diesel electric locomotive at 34 ft long is comfortably accommodated in the trailer well, pictured in October 1953 en route from Rugby to Australia via Liverpool docks. One of the drawbacks of being so low to the ground is aptly demonstrated by the outfit pictured totally grounded on a slight hill peak.*

were not without their problems. In fact it took until 1938 before the established London heavy haulier of E. W. Rudd Ltd publicly declared that in their opinion the use of steam vehicles for heavy haulage work was out of date. Rudds had been one of Scammells first customers in the early 1920s but it had taken the elapse of a further eighteen years before they finally withdrew from service their last Fowler tractor. The need for frequent refuelling with coal and water was what Rudds felt was the main disadvantage of steam power. Long journeys for the steamers meant the necessity for support vehicles carrying fuel for the boiler to accompany the load. Rudds were finding that the steamers couldn't even cross London in one night due to their slow average speed brought about by these regular refuelling stops. Rudds made the transition to what we consider to be fairly conventional Scammell ballasted tractors although Pickfords persisted with their big Fowlers inherited from companies like Norman E. Box and London Traction Haulage, for their heavy traffic.

DYW 817 was an experimental tractor built for Pickfords, the large rear wheels tend to give away the fact that it was built by McLarens of Leeds, a company steeped in steamer history. Seen manoeuvring in the works of C. A. Parsons on 17 February 1939, the load of a 68-ton stator destined for New South Wales railways is being supported on NB35, the old Norman E. Box Fowler trailer.

Their Scammell 100-ton artic BLH 21 was kept very busy so it seems strange that when they did move away from steam they went to J. & H. McLaren Ltd, Midland Engine Works, Leeds 10 for some special tractors.

McLaren had achieved considerable success with the steam traction engine so it is perhaps understandable that when they did produce their first experimental diesel tractor unit it was based entirely on the lines of a massive traction engine. DYW 617 was its registration and unless you knew what it was, it was difficult to even hazard a guess. The subsequent production unit did in fact look like a truck, with a conventional cab mounted at the front although the McLaren-Ricardo 5 MR diesel engine which produced 125 bhp at 1,000 rpm was mounted midships behind the cab. With only an 11-ft wheelbase it meant the four-speed gearbox was mounted directly above the rear axle thus the transmission was very compact. Although the McLaren offered 24-volt electric starting and twin fuel

Chris Miller's ARN 453 is an example of how big a varience there can be in the choice of ballasted tractors. This was originally designed as an airport tug for the RAF by David Browns, but having water-filled tyres for ballast and a winch meant that Miller's pressed it into a great deal of use including hauling this 15-ft Hands trailer.

Opposite above *Civilian use of the Thornycroft Antar was quite a rarity, but XMT 586 was an example specially built for this purpose and was only 9 ft wide. It had a Rover Meteorite diesel engine and was bought by Hill from Sir Robert McAlpine. The 40-ton dynamontre car (a converted Churchill tank) was hauled on a 60-ton Rogers tank transporter to Christchurch by driver Jack Murphy during 1967.*

Opposite middle *The armed forces had been the trail blazers in advocating articulated vehicles for use as tank transporters. This Scammell Pioneer outfit is seen during trials in the mid-1930s carrying a Cruiser Mk I battle tank used both by the British Expeditionary Force in 1939 and in the Western Desert campaign of 1940-41.*

Opposite below *In civilian use the heavy haulier tended to convert the semi-trailer into drawbar use although a far greater carrying capacity was normally demanded from it. Wynn's famous 100-ton Foden is seen hauling this 9-ft 8-in wide Shelvoke and Drewry trailer. The pushing Pioneer is fleet number 140, registration number DDW 495.*

tanks of a total capacity of 125 gallons, what gave its pedigree away was that the solid-tyred rubber rear wheels were 6 ft in diameter and 16 in wide. True the front wheels of 3 ft diameter and 8 in width were on pneumatics but Pickfords' M3933 was really dated in its concept.

The McLaren could certainly pull its weight grossing 109 tons on one of its early runs from Birmingham to London. It nearly managed 1 mph although unladen top speed was rather leisurely by modern-day standards at an approximate 9.82 mph. The McLaren was probably never destined to succeed for its launch in 1941 coincided with the arrival of the Diamond T tank transporters from the USA, a marque the big heavy hauliers quickly snapped up whenever they could lay their hands on them. However the civilian hauliers tended to use them in ballasted form, which was rather surprising as their Army counterparts nearly always used them in articulated form. This line of practice was what the development of the heavy articulated vehicle was up against although one of its early problems slowing growth was its fifth-wheel coupling. It should be remembered that early artics were not built to uncouple, in fact it was the direct opposite as sometimes manufacturers were at pains to emphasize that these were not trailers that were being hauled. Thus the early version of the artic was more like a rigid that hinged in the centre, for separation of the two parts was a major workshops' operation.

There was still a place for them as Sunters found first hauling long timber and then long steel from Cargoe Fleet in Middlesbrough to the central London stockyard. With no form of vertical oscillation in these crude fifth wheels it meant that the trailer had to withstand the heavy shocks due to the unending flexing and distorting between the tractor chassis and the trailer wheels as the outfit drove along. Obviously the longer the trailer, the greater the flexing and distorting. The wooden pole trailer was certainly very handy in some respects but it couldn't always take these distortions as Sunter driver Jack Stout found when he was heading north up the A1 near Boroughbridge one day. The long descent down past Kelly's Cafe found him grappling with the outfit and juggling with the trailer brake as he endeavoured to slow down before the town itself. With an almighty crack the pole snapped and although it fell to the ground it continued on at the same speed, ran underneath the rear of the braking tractor and simply lifted the back axle up off the ground, high and dry as it came to a grinding halt.

Fellow Sunter driver John Robinson also related another story where the length of the pole, which projected beyond the rear of the trailer running gear, was a factor in saving his outfit from getting substantially damaged. Anyone having delivered to the Dunlop and Ranken steel stockyard on the outskirts of Leeds will know that the entrance is a sharp left off the main road followed by a steep climb up to the premises. Parking it in gear with all the brakes on, John left his pole artic to find out about unloading. He was thus helpless when the brakes failed and the outfit started to run backwards down the hill. It crossed the main road, fortunately without hitting anybody, but the force of impact on the adjacent wall was all taken on the projecting

Opposite top *Sunter Bros were early operators of the pole semi-trailer artic. DPY 447 is coupled to a Northallerton-built unit although it had running gear made by the Manchester Trailer Company. The ERF was owned twice by the North Yorks haulier, but it is seen here in Pickfords colours during the period of nationalization. Bob Caygill is at the wheel.*

Opposite middle *A more substantial pole semi-trailer is supporting this storage tank being tended to by Leslie Taylor and Pat Dodsworth prior to leaving Distington Engineering in 1964. The well-turned-out left-hand-drive Leyland Super Hippo was renowned to be quite a fly machine although its brakes never really coped with the speed it could travel at.*

Opposite bottom *Seen in this Dow Mac photograph, the pole semi-trailer was specially built for the haulier Septimus Cook by fabricating engineers Wright, Anderson & Co of Gateshead. There were 29 tons of the 68-ft long post-tensioned concrete beam hauled from Tallington to Cheshire during 1963, destined for Bridge 19 on the Crewe to Birdswood line.*

pole which prevented any damage to the rest of the vehicle or its load. The wall was substantial enough to bounce the artic forward, which in turn fired the engine into life so that the driverless vehicle then tried to climb back up the hill from where it came, or so John would have us believe.

This incident apart, the wooden pole was not really a total success and at least one north-eastern driver lost his life when his broken pole came through the back of the cab. Conversant with this last tragic incident, Bill Foster the managing director of A. Stevens & Co of Great Ayton, North Yorkshire, specialists in long steel carriage, taxed his mind to the problem. The solution that he produced was both simple and effective.

If you look at any drawbar-trailer outfit, no matter what age, you will see that the freedom given to both drawing vehicle and its trailer is because they are only loosely connected to each other. Each part of the outfit can move around to a large degree, in a vertical plane, totally independent of the other, the free-moving drawbar being only really required to pull or push the trailer along. Using these thoughts in relation to a pole artic, the Stevens solution was not to join the pole to the crude fifth-wheel turntable but simply to hitch the pole, drawbar fashion, to the rear of the tractor chassis. In essence this wasn't an artic but simply a drawbar-trailer outfit, albeit with a very long drawbar. The trailer bogie could still be made to slide up and down the pole so there was no versatility lost in the exercise, but it meant the end of the flexing for the trailer pole. Stevens operated this idea quite successfully with their pole artics, and it was only superseded with the arrival of the modern type of oscillating fifth-wheel coupling that we know today.

One item of technology which was also slow to develop a better product for both artics and tractor/trailer combinations was that of pneumatic tyres. The first heavy haulage versions were based on those developed from bomber aircraft, and were rather big and bulbous in nature. Scammells were keen advocates of these super singles, as was Tom Sunter who converted all his semi-trailers to this type, although many of his drivers cursed him for making this decision. Once they blew out, and you soon knew about that, they were hell to change. It was all right getting the spare down on to the road but how do you get the punctured one back up 4 ft on to the trailer platform? Brute strength alone was no good but overhanging tree branches were a driver's best friend. Utilizing a rope over the bough and tied to the back of the lorry, forward movement lifted the

Above *At first sight ex-army EVN 611 may seem just a normal type of articulated vehicle, but the location at the headboard gives away the fact that it is hauling a drawbar rather than a semi-trailer. The concept was devised by A. Stevens & Co to combat the high breakage level created in long-length pole-trailer artics.*

Below *With conventional suspension only, this King semi-trailer was never fully utilized by Sunters even though they shortened the length of the well to make it more acceptable for their type of work. If you think this bucket is big you ought to see the crane that lifts it! NAJ 102P is seen leaving Sunters' depot in mid-1978 with its 35-ton load destined to be attached to the extended arm of the infamous 'Big Geordie'.*

tyre so that it could be swung on board. If there wasn't a tree handy you tied the rope to the lorry and simply dragged the heavy tyre along until you found one. For really heavy weights the solid-tyred load-carrying trailers reigned supreme until well into the 1950s whilst the solid-tyred bogies lasted even longer, due mainly to their strength and low running height. Even in 1985 Pickfords still admitted to having a set at Glasgow, albeit mainly for internal work.

Cranes of Dereham, Norfolk seemed to lead the development in both girder trailers and bogies for as the 1950s raced by loads of up to 200 tons were being talked about and even moved. This was no domain for the artic—the ballasted tractor reigned supreme for no matter how heavy the load you just had to add a few tractors on to the front and the combined efforts would see you through, no matter what the terrain. The technique of double, triple or quadruple heading up still requires a great deal of concentration for being the lead driver of so many tractors can be quite a daunting prospect as 'Coconut Joe' Whillis would testify.

He headed such a line up of tractors pulling a 212-ton vessel up the infamous Cut Bank, at Byker, Newcastle one day and was fairly worried about not letting anyone down. The senior driver on the line instructed him what gear to select but emphasized whatever happened that he must not ease off before the top of the incline was reached. Joe selected gear, the order to go was given, the clutch was let out with a thump, the throttle banged to the floor and the tractor leapt away. Joe never flinched, his eyes stuck to the road, intently concentrating on steering as straight a line as possible. With the diesel bellowing hard in his ears he made the top without any problem. The only thing wrong was that his fellow drivers, and the load of course, were still at the bottom of the hill! Joe had taken off with such a leap that the pin connecting him to the next tractor had jumped up allowing the drawbar to be pulled free. Joe had certainly followed his instructions to the letter, although he did have his leg pulled about this for some time after.

When any steep descent was encountered the additional tractors were added on to the rear where they were able to act as extra braking ballast, thus any long-distance heavy haulage involving two tractors over varying terrain found them normally in pull-push combination. With the trailer and its load separating the drivers it was essential that some form of direct communication linked the two tractors. When Hopes of Bedfont, Middlesex were moving 100-ft concrete beams for Kingsbury they had a small pushing AEC Mercury tractor mainly for

Above *Double heading is an age old technique that can be used with ballasted tractors. This Hill outfit is seen clawing up Beacon Hill on the A34 at Whitchurch, Hampshire about 1960. The 60-ton Lima crawler is being carried on a 60-ton Crane float trailer fitted with 16.00 × 20 24 ply tyres. Bill Miles is alongside TOT 297, an old Explorer, which is partially concealing Pioneer KXT 872 with a similar Scammell pushing at the rear.*

Below *This line up of Pickfords' was ready for the harrowing descent to Rugeley power station during 1960. The Junior Constructor, two Constructors and Diamond T at the rear were mainly to act as braking ballast. The 150-ton load is supported on the Crane 200-ton capacity trailer which had the fleet numbers 413 and 5261.*

steering the rear bogie. Inter-driver communication on that day was in the form of two adapted baby alarms—even being able to give a simple buzz can make all the difference at the time as some of Sunters' men will tell you.

Jimmy Goulding was driving his Cummins-powered left-hand-drive Diamond T one day with a Foden 100 tonner pushing at the rear. Anyone who has driven a vehicle with this type of engine will know that one slight difference of the Cummins is that it is fitted with an electric fuel pump so if there is an electrical failure, such as a blown fuse, the diesel pump stops and the engine cuts out. Such a failure happened as the load was going down Piccadilly, Manchester and the resultant loss of power brought everything to a halt. In a fit of temper Jimmy whipped the door open and in two strides via the massive running board he was down on to the pavement ready to lift the bonnet and remedy the problem. Unfortunately the pushing Foden wasn't aware of what was going on and, thinking that more effort was required, the driver simply gave the old girl the boot which resulted in forward progress once more. Such a slight stoppage isn't unknown in the heavy haulage world but the Foden crew did think it rather peculiar that the pedestrian they passed jumping up and down in frustration should in fact have been driving the leading tractor!

As the ballasted tractor continued to pull more and more weight,

With an all-up weight close to 350 tons, Hill of Botley were asked to assist Wynn's in the cross-country movement of this transformer train from Fleet to Portsmouth during March 1970. The strange double-pulling formation was adopted during manoeuvring in Wickham Square on the A353 prior to an overnight halt. PUC 474, driven by George Holbrook, started life with Pickfords as fleet number 1010.

his small articulated cousin was undergoing a total revolution. The four-in-line low loader had lasted well but its capacity for weight was always going to be limited. Six-wheeled tractors were used and sometimes two sets of four wheels in line were utilized but it needed a complete turn round in design before better acceptance of the artic could be made in the heavy-weight league.

Up until the 1950s it was the rear axles which were always the portion of the trailer that was removed to allow access to the loading area. But when it was realized that if the swan neck was made detachable instead of these rear wheels then the articulated low loader took on an entirely fresh way of use. Initially separation was done in a similar manner to the knock-out rear in that side jacks were used to support the front of the trailer before locking pins were removed. This freed the swan neck while still being attached to the tractor unit so it was now just a matter of driving the vehicle out of the way whilst loading was going on. The big advantage of this idea was that the trailer bogie which was now fixed to the load-carrying frame could take the form of a well-tried and relatively cheap to produce tandem-axled bogie which was common to most straight-frame general haulage platform trailers. This type of suspension was a lot lighter, it was well served from the spare parts point of view and could of course be operated on identical wheel and tyre equipment to that used on the tractive unit.

Another technique regularly adopted by ballasted tractor drivers was nose pining. Turning the tractor round meant the driver could see what he was doing much more easily. DVN 231 was mainly used on internal work by ICI and is pictured in the movement of a small pipe bridge at Wilton works during 1959.

Opposite top left *To move this 45-ton, 20-ft high boiler on 8 November 1959 from Woolston, Southampton to the Admiralty Fuel Experimental station at Haslar, Hill of Botley used an interesting low-loading trailer. Built by Eagle, originally for McAlpines, with a capacity of 60 tons, the rear tandem four-in-line axles on 14.00 × 20 single tyres could be knocked out to assist with loading. Police Officer Ron Harris is supervising traffic whilst the driver of the hauling Pioneer, Gordon Prebble has nipped off for a mid-morning breakfast.*

Opposite top right *The problem created by concentrated weight on low loaders is aptly demonstrated with this Siddle C. Cook outfit seen in Yarm Road, Stockton on 30 March 1953. It proved no problem for the sturdy Foden, but the 32-ton Riley boiler has broken the back of the Boys semi-trailer not far from the manufacturer's works.*

Opposite middle *It was quite a change of concept for the articulated low loader when it was designed to have the front swan neck removable to allow access to the well, rather than knocking out the rear axles. RVN 569H was one of the first Scania six-wheelers used by Sunters and was photographed by Alan Simpson about to leave Head Wrightson at Thornaby on 13 April 1972. Driver Albert Lowes was to deliver this Treadwell hot metal carrier to Llanwern in South Wales.*

Opposite bottom *The design of the step-frame semi-trailer has varied little with the passage of time although better design and engineering has produced a stronger product. The Crane tri-axle version had a 40-ft long carrying area and was an ideal fit for this 36-ton Caterpillar during 1973. The Foden tractor was well liked by driver Bill Lloyd although he recalls the necessity for 28 gear changes up one testing incline due to a slight lack of power from the 180 Gardner at heavy haulage work.*

Below *A. Stevens & Co of Great Ayton operated two of these Power Plus Leyland Octopus eight-wheelers on long-load work in the early 1960s, together with other strange types of tractive units including Albion Reivers and a Scammell Routeman. Stevens were obliged to use the tipper specification vehicles due to a lack of suitably strong multi-wheeled artic tractors for their type of work.*

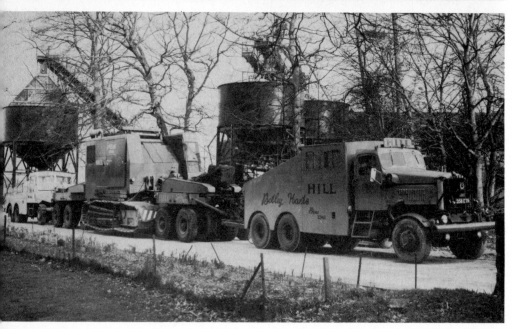

Opposite top *One tractor which has experienced life both in articulated and ballasted form is the well-travelled Foden, MPT 527. Starting off coupled to a semi-trailer working for Crook and Willington Carriers, it then passed to Siddle Cook of Consett who operated it in both forms. David James bought the 6 × 4 tractor from Rush Green Motors of Hitchin for his company of Wrekin Roadways and after having a new ballast box fitted it worked under contract to Adamson Alliance of Horsehay. The outfit is en route to South Wales in 1960 with this crane girder, the Pickfords Highwayman being utilized for steering the rearmost solid-tyred Crane bogie.*

Opposite below *The girder trailer was the standard outfit used to carry heavy crawler plant when the load carrier had been drawn in to its navvy width of only 4 ft 6 in. Hill's 110-ton capacity unit is supporting an 80-ton Marion crane that was taken from Washington, Sussex to Chichester in 1968. The pushing Junior Constructor is 874 AUU, which formerly belonged to Marples Ridgeway & Partners of Watford.*

Below *For smaller loads the artic was a viable alternative for crawler machines. This Dyson semi operated by Goodfellows of Manchester offered a capacity of 75 tons and a well length of 28 ft. The rear bogie was highly manoeuvrable and it also incorporated hydraulic suspension via its own power pack. This particular trailer was made so that both front and rear swan necks could be removed from the bed.*

The next step on from the change of removable ends was to build in a hydraulic jacking system to the swan neck assembly itself thus disconnecting the need for hand-operated side jacks. Both uncoupling and coupling up the trailer could now be done in minutes, thus enhancing the articulated low loader even more. The company of D. H. Morgan were one of the first in the United Kingdom to offer this type of device with their hydro-couple swan neck although they were soon bought out by Highway Trailers of Southampton who in turn were absorbed into the Crane Fruehauf Group based in Norfolk. King Trailers Ltd of Market Harborough also claim that they were the forerunners of this device with their version called the hydro neck which they introduced from North America. Not so popular however was the idea that the swan neck, or goose neck as it was sometimes called, was made to fold flat, its structure thus forming an easy-access ramp on to the loading deck proper.

One problem which has stayed with the artic for its entire existence is that of excess weight being carried on the tractor unit in general and on its drive axles in particular. Stevens of Great Ayton were one company who tried a variation of tractor units to combat this problem for their long load work. 252 AVN, 260 FAJ and 321 FVN were six-wheeled Albion Reiver tractors, 820 EVN an eight-wheeled Scammell Routeman and 864 FAJ and 863 FAJ were similar four-axled Power Plus Leyland Octopuses. Unfortunately even these converted tipper specification units weren't strong enough and the chassis tended to crack due to the heavy imposed load.

The heavy hauliers were thus once again a confused band of men. It was clear that for loads in excess of 100 tons the ballasted tractor/trailer combination was unbeatable. It was also clear that if your big loads only weighed 10 or 15 tons then an articulated low loader would certainly fit the bill. But if your traffic varied somewhere between these two weight bands then you just had to opt for one or the other and it was interesting to see which way operators went when confronted with this choice. Articulated units seemed to be the most popular and even the big crawler machines which used to be only carried on small girder-frame trailers squeezed down to their 4 ft 6 in 'navvy' width were now being hauled on 'beefed up' artics.

Chris Miller of Croft Street, Preston were a family-based company and it is only recently that they have reached the real heavyweight league of operations, although in the 1950s their big acquisition was HCK 321 a 4 × 2 Scammell box tractor. At the time the company thought they had really made it, at last a tractor just like that used by

Above and below *Chris Miller thought they had really made it when HCK 321 joined the fleet, at last they had a 25-ton tractor just like Pickfords and Wynn's (above). Unfortunately it didn't last long in ballast tractor form, it being more practical to convert it for use as an artic (below). Bob Baron is hand winching the small shunting engine on to the low loader at Lostock Hall gas works, the pair of knock-out axles being removed to allow for easy access.*

The first type of coffin carrier operated by British Nuclear Fuels in West Cumbria was a special ERF-Dyson articulated combination which ran at a gross weight of approximately 73 tons. Seen leaving Chapelcross, the Rolls-Royce-powered outfit was used until 1970 but the configuration was changed to that of a ballasted Scammell-drawbar outfit. BNFL currently run two MAN Jumbo 32.400s on the same work hauling Crane Fruehauf drawbar trailers, all-up weight being approximately 94 tons.

Pickfords and Wynns. The Scammell certainly lived up to its rating of being able to haul 25-ton abnormal loads, the only thing was when it was carrying more routine bales of wool, the heavy 14-ton unladen weight of the tractor/trailer combination brought its legal payload down to only 10 tons which wasn't really economically viable. It thus wasn't long before the ballast box was chopped off and a fifth wheel coupling substituted in its place.

British Nuclear Fuels of Sellafield, however, was one operator who went the other way, for in 1958 YSM 351, a rather special articulated low loader, took to the road. The ERF 6 × 4 tractor unit was powered by a Rolls-Royce C6NFR engine producing 200 bhp and a maximum 548 lb/ft torque from its 12.17 litres, with its five-speed gearbox coupled to a two-speed epicyclic auxiliary box giving ten forward speeds and a top speed capability of 25 mph. Carrying the 50-ton radioactive payload was a Dyson semi-trailer which, unlike most low-loading semi-trailers, was of fixed construction with neither the swan neck nor the two sets of four-wheels-in-line rear bogies being detachable. With only a 13-ft long well, the overall length of this outfit was 49 ft, its normal gross running weight being 73 tons.

The articulated low loader served BNFL well but when it came up for renewal in 1970 it was replaced by TSM 65H and TSM 66H, two Scammell Contractor ballasted tractors hauling similar flasks on a Crane Fruehauf drawbar trailer. The reason for this change was said to be that the excise licence per vehicle was cheaper for the drawbar outfit and it was said to be able to do the same job at a much reduced cost. This seems a reasonable line of thought but hauling similar

To get the best of both worlds many heavy hauliers now run heavyweight articulated tractor units which can be converted by the fitment of a temporary ballast box. Dennis Harris found this Pickfords S26 40-35 hauling Nicolas axles about to loose its packaged load to the M V Starman Africa *at North Shields during June 1985.*

The modern fleet of Wrekin Transport Services normally runs in articulated form but to haul this 130-ft long, 40-ton crane girder, the haulier preferred to do the haul in locomotive form. There is 20 tons of ballast in the box which is a converted ex-War Department Bedford tipper body. John Smith, crewed by Bill Lewis and Phillip Franks, is seen on the M5 in Gloucestershire en route from AB Cranes at Telford to Avonmouth docks. The load is destined for export to China.

coffins out of Hinckley Point Power Station in 1982 were GTC 603X and GTC 621X, two Scammell S24 tractive units coupled to tandem-axle Crane Fruehauf semi-trailers. The latest offering from Scammell had a 326 bhp Cummins engine and Allison automatic transmission, the vehicles coming to Hinckley Point to replace a ballasted Foden S75 6 × 4 tractor and drawbar trailer combination.

The choice between the ballasted tractor and the artic can now boil down to personal preference for the passage of time has certainly seen the artic come of age as the modern-day version is certainly more comparable to the old established ballasted tractor. Unless it is guaranteed that you will always be moving loads of three figures worth of weight and more, then the artic seems the best choice, provided you can improvise things with the fitting of a temporary ballast box when the really heavy weights have to be moved. In heavy haulage improvisation is nearly always the name of the game.

Chapter 3

Improvisation and the law

It would be a utopian state of affairs in the heavy haulage world if, no matter what the load you were asked to move, you had an outfit just waiting in the yard that would carry it ideally. True the standard type of modern-day low loader can accept a variety of castings, machines, transformers or boilers with natural ease but when it comes down to something a bit longer, a bit heavier, a bit higher or even something more susceptible to damage in transit, then heavy hauliers have to adapt whatever they have, fabricate it into something they want and perhaps reluctantly buy something which they can't procure through any other means. If you sort through any heavy haulier's tackle you will find an accumulation of bits and pieces possibly dating back to the time they started in business. It is not considered to be miserly, but merely good business practice, to keep using something in one form or another which, as far as the accountancy books are concerned, was written off as being of no value years ago.

It is worth remembering that only twenty years ago the general haulier could only operate up to 24 tons gross combination weight with a maximum trailer length, on the few artics that were in use, of 25 ft. This was when the regulations limited the overall length of normal artics to 35 ft although there has always been some form of general dispensation to this overall length limit for vehicles which were manufactured and normally used for the carriage of loads of exceptional length. It was the long steel carriers of the day who tended to use this type of trailer—in the early 1960s I can recall seeing, with an air of disbelief, 984 ALP, a well-turned-out Leyland Beaver four-axled artic belonging to Davis Bros (Haulage) Ltd of London, fleet number 1013, coupled to a 40-ft Dyson platform semi-trailer. The outfit seemed so rare at the time that I felt obliged to record it on film for posterity.

Above *When you have to carry a 49-ft 6-in long propellor shaft on a low loader that measures no more than 20 ft in the well, your technique has to be improvised, the method being demonstrated with this ERF of the Sunderland Forge & Engineering Company. The 14-ton load was destined for export to Davie Shipbuilding of Canada.*

Below *The eight-wheeled rigid had a natural air of strength about it and found itself recruited to haul many heavy loads of the day. This Gateshead Leyland is destined for Kent in 1952 with this 12-ton, 31-ft long boiler. The C disc displayed on the side window denotes that it was only licensed to carry Clarke Chapman's own products.*

Above *It should be remembered that although 40-ft platform semi-trailers are close to being the norm in the 1980s, twenty years earlier they were quite a rarity. This well-turned-out Beaver is coupled to a Dyson semi-trailer and is weighing off on the plate bridge at Consett Iron Company about 1961.*

Below *The technique of improvisation is aptly shown both in the design of this Box outfit and in the method used to negotiate this tight turn in Brecon about 1938. The hauling locomotive is Fowler No 17106, registration KD 2826, whilst the semi-trailer is easily recognizable as being that normally used with Box's Scammell 100-ton artic. The pushing Scammell was bought by Box from the Newcastle Electric Supply Company who had used it mostly for off-the-road work.*

Being manufactured under licence by W. G. Armstrong-Whitworth Co Ltd of Newcastle, it was natural that the Swiss Saurer found favour with north-eastern operators. Currie's eight-wheeler Samson, fleet number 200 was well thought of by its drivers, having the rarity of being fitted with an all-wheel air braking system. BTN 588 is about to leave for the Northampton Electric Light and Power Company with this 10-ton storage tank in September 1935.

The long-length artic was certainly a rare outfit, but more commonplace was the rigid eight-wheeler which also was permitted to gross 24 tons all-up weight. Its overall length was restricted to a maximum of 30 ft but with not having to bend in the middle, nor even the hint of being fitted with a sleeper cab, its usable platform body length was

normally very close to that of the artic of 25 ft. The eight-wheeler had
the air of a more substantial build than its counterpart artic, and of
course it was more common, so it naturally found itself pressed into
use to carry some substantial loads of the day. In fact rather than
invest in expensive extended-length semi-trailers to move any long
loads in a highly efficient and safe manner, hauliers preferred to chop
down trucks that had been laid to rest years ago and convert their
running gear into made-to-measure bogies.

Frank Annis, whose company of Annis & Co Ltd operated out of
Pump Lane, Hayes, Middlesex, did such a good modification making
some substantial bogies from old tank transporters that he decided to
protect the idea by patent which reflects the attitude the heavy
haulier has towards his handiwork. Virtually everything that came
into the Annis fleet was modified in some way or another, including
the fitting of Gardner engines into an AEC Mammoth Major eight-
wheeler and Diamond T 6 x 4 tractors. Annis also made his own tower
jacks out of Bedford QL axles but it was mainly the articles with
wheels on that got most pressed into use.

The platform wagon hauling an independent bogie may not be a

*The concept of platform wagons hauling long loads supported on independent
bogies was well used, its acceptance being shown in this Distington Engineering
photograph taken during the 1950s. Even BRS preferred to improvise with their
own load carriers rather than hand over the traffic to the special loads division of
Pickfords.*

Septimus Cook never built a fleet up as large as his more famous brother and he preferred to drive his own truck on long load work. MPT 375 was a right-hand-drive Canadian Dodge with a P6 Perkins engine and is seen on John Street Square at Consett in October 1953. When not loosely coupled to a pole semi-trailer, the Dodge was used with a small tipping body on local quarry work.

common sight today but its acceptance is reflected in the fact that even some branches of British Road Services operated this type of configuration rather than hand their long loads to the special traffics division of Pickfords. There were times when even a bogie wasn't required as Septimus Cook, the seventh son of Consett haulier Thomas Cook and brother to Siddle C. Cook, used to show.

Sepy never expanded operations to the size of the more famous Cook's fleet and he eventually sold out to Stillers of Darlington in 1967 to go in for clearing house work. The three vehicles he used in the 1960s were an Atkinson, 789 GPT, a Guy Invincible, 3456 PT, and a Leyland Beaver, 7766 UP, all on long-length work, but his personal pride must have been *Lady Mary*, Foden SPT 403, which he ran until 1962. Originally a 1938 model, it was bought and refurbished from the local cattle carrier Parky Bates of Iveston. Although it was only capable of 32 mph at top speed, Sepy still reckoned that he did 1,500 to 2,000 miles per week on long-load work which meant his was a hard eleven-hour day six days a week. He did not however engage in one particular pastime related by some long-length artic drivers running out of Teesside who should perhaps remain nameless.

On running home empty up the A1 from London, they often took pity on a fellow north-easterner driving a lone AEC which had originally started life as a drawbar tractor with Consett Iron

Company, but on changing hands had been converted into an artic although its top speed of 23 mph wasn't modified so even on good stretches of dual carriageway progress was rather slow. In contrast the Gardner 6LX 150 bhp-powered Foden with suitable gearing could do 40 mph so, provided the rear of the semi-trailer being hauled at the time was compatible, the Foden used to push the empty AEC which had its gear stick in neutral up to nearly twice its normal capability. When a roundabout or town was reached the Foden simply eased off and allowed the AEC to negotiate it under its own power, the pushing recommencing once the hazard was cleared. Running by himself Sepy never indulged in that excitement although his way of operation was sometimes quite different itself.

Lady Mary was normally coupled to a pole semi-trailer capable of perhaps 40- or 50-ft loads as it stood. For longer lengths, like some 90-ft piling bars that were taken from Teesside to Bradwell in Essex, the trailer was simply unhitched and used as a bogie supporting the load towards the rear. The pole was simply left stretching half-way down the load but as it was correctly aligned and secured nothing could go wrong. This also is not a practice seen often today, perhaps because

Sepy Cook's most remembered tractor was this Foden SPT 403 which he called Lady Mary. The Dow Mac 22 ton concrete beam was 74-ft long and one of fifteen hauled by Cook from Tallington to St Athans, South Wales. When stopped in Ross on Wye once by his police escort, when carrying a similar load, Sepy recalls a woman driver going straight under the load without touching it and oblivious to anything at all untoward having occurred.

Above *To move this 50-ft long, 6-ft diameter, 12-ton rotary dryer from Lancashire to Darlington in 1937, Chris Miller used their new TSC 9 Leyland Beaver and trailer for the job. The most difficult part of the journey was near to the start and the crew are power steering the outfit on to the main road just outside the Hoo Hill brickworks at Blackpool.*

Below *Miller's four-wheeled ERF, ACK 853, found itself without its platform body quite often. It is seen here acting in the role of a strange type of tractor. It hauled this 15-ton section of the Mulberry Harbour from Southampton to Preston in about 1947 where Colonel Bustard was to use it in the construction of the first ro-ro berth in the United Kingdom.*

through the passage of time man has gained experience in how to move things.

Millers of Preston weren't exceptionally heavy hauliers in 1937 but when they were asked to move what was described as an 'abnormal indivisible load'—a 50-ft long, 6-ft diameter, 12-ton rotary dryer from Blackpool to Darlington they simply used their new TSC9 Leyland Beaver Six and drawbar trailer for the job. Just to clarify matters, the Beaver was a four-wheeler and the combined platform lengths of this wagon and drag, which was more used to moving more gentle bales of wool, would be no more than 30 ft, but Millers hauled the load without a hitch. Millers found the cylinder resting on its side on two supporting pillars at the Hoo Hill brickworks. Loading was done in the traditional manner by simply rolling the cylinder over level planks straight on to swivelling bolsters which were mounted over the rear axle of the Beaver and midway down the trailer. Like most hauls, the difficult part of the job was making the 90° turn out of the brickworks on to the main road. This was achieved by steering the drawbar trailer by two-man power after it was unhitched from the pulling Beaver. Millers did a lot of timber work at that time so to unload they utilized the forest method of a tripod and block and tackle. The cylinder was then rolled over 50 ft of ground and lowered by the same method to a trench especially prepared for it.

The term 'abnormal indivisible load' is a legal expression although at times it is abbreviated so that the heavy haulage industry simply refers to abnormal loads. The word indivisible may be left out but as far as the law is concerned it is just as important as the word abnormal. A 100-ton load of building bricks is certainly quite large but as it can be divided down into individual bricks, then as far as heavy haulage is concerned it is not an abnormal load. The legal definition was first used in the Motor Vehicles (Authorization of Special Types) Order 1931 and is still in general usage today. At the time an 'abnormal indivisible load' meant a load which (a) could not without undue expense or risk of damage be divided into two or more loads for the purpose of conveyance on a road and (b) could not owing to its dimensions or weight be carried by a motor vehicle or trailer complying in all respects with the requirements of the Motor Vehicles Construction and Use Regulations 1931.

You will see that nowhere in that legal mouthful does it say in practical terms what an abnormal load really is. The first part about being just one item is fairly easy to comprehend but what does it mean about being able to be carried on a vehicle and comply with the normal regulations? You might wonder why all the discussion over a

few sentences, although to the modern-day heavy haulier under-
standing of the law is just as important as making the choice between
an artic or ballasted tractor/trailer combination. For if you are carrying
such an abnormal indivisible load, then the regulations relating to
weight, width and length are relaxed. Since they were introduced in
1967, the Plating and Testing regulations have not applied to motor
vehicles and trailers used solely for this line of work so consequently
the old equipment does not have the problem of passing this yearly
rigorous examination and its life expectancy is that much longer.
Conversely if your load is not classified as coming under the legal
definition of being an 'abnormal' one, then the outfit is considered to
be just another normal haulage vehicle and all the regulations which
apply to those are enforceable.

One area where heavy hauliers regularly transgress the regulations
is in the movement of ancillary pieces along with their main load.
They may be asked to move a large 50-ton boiler for instance which
can be quite legally carried because that sort of weight obviously
means it is an abnormal load. But if they add a couple of crated boxes
containing valves, brackets or even the boiler chimney dismantled
into several pieces, then carrying this along with the boiler on the
same vehicle is, according to the regulations, unlawful. These stress
that the vehicle may only be used 'for or in connection with the
carriage of an abnormal indivisible load', although the hauliers do
find sympathy occasionally in this not unreasonable carriage of extra
items.

McKelvies of Glasgow were prosecuted in 1964 after one of their
vehicles was stopped because as well as carrying an indivisible
elevator and hopper mechanism, it was also carrying certain equipment taken from the elevator and hopper and just lying on the floor of
the vehicle. The total weight of the vehicle so loaded was 28 tons and
even without the loose pieces would still have weighed more than the
24 tons allowed for normal heavy goods vehicles under the
Construction and Use regulations, thus it was carrying an abnormal
load, albeit with extra pieces. However in emphasizing that
McKelvies were legally at fault, Lord C. J. Parker said, 'I am sorry for
hauliers in these circumstances, it seems so eminently reasonable
that some small items of equipment which can be dismantled should
be carried in the same vehicle. However if one extended the meaning
of the words to cover that, it is difficult to see where one would stop.'

This concept of carrying only one item had some strange spin offs,
not least of which was demonstrated in the carriage of crawler cranes
and drag lines. As standard these machines were fitted with long

Above *Known as* Smokey *to the Siddle Cook crew, RUP 900 is seen at BSC Lackenby prior to a testing haul to Hownsgill at Consett during 1956. The 110-ft long crane girder is supported on two 24-wheeled tank transporters joined together by a telescopic drawbar. With 65 tons of payload the Gardner-engined* Mountaineer *was under pressure and driver Jimmy Brown required double heading up the fierce Leven and Jaw Blades inclines.*

Below *Originally built as a ballasted tractor, Siddle Cook demanded that SPT 600 took on a varying type of role converting it as and when desired to a 100-ton artic. Driver's mate Bob Cook is posed for the camera, the photographer being the outfit driver Walter Tomlinson. This crew took the 65-ton stator outer casing on a local cross-Tyneside haul from the makers, Palmers, to the recipients at Parsons.*

Above *The standard heavy haulage outfit for middleweight traffic in the 1950s was the ballasted tractor and float drawbar trailer, so named as it simply floated along behind the drawing unit. Hallett's Junior Constructor is coupled to a Crane unit offering 60-ton capacity on its eight rather large tyres, a rating which would be considered horrific thirty years later. Some indication of the weight of each wheel, and thus their strength, is shown by the need for a lifting arm on the trailer neck to facilitate transfer.*

Below *The concern of overloading the articulated tractive unit has always been a major worry to heavy hauliers but finding a traditionally-configured eight-wheeler in this modern day role is a rare sight. Dave Lee found Van De Vlist's well-turned-out Dutch-built FTF on the A30 in Cornwall during 1984 close to the end of a long haul from Germany. The 14-ft wide Demag base machine is supported on a Nooteboom semi-trailer and destined for use with EEC Quarries Ltd.*

Above *Driver Peter Clarke is seen negotiating Piccadily Circus close to midnight with one of about twelve very unusual loads that Sunters hauled from Brentford to the then new London Transport Museum at Covent Garden. This LCC EI-type tramcar was built at Leytonstone in 1910 and finally withdrawn from service in 1952, 27 years later it crossed the capital sitting on a 20-ton capacity King extendable. AVN 311T, as its headboard suggests, was more than often to be found hauling on the southern side of the English Channel.*

Below *There was no stopping Dave Yates as he made this awkward turn on to Borough Road, Middlesborough on Sunday 14 April 1985. He had taken five days to haul this 17-ft wide, 18-ft high marine underwater plough from Birkenhead, but was close to his destination at Haverton Hill. YRN 431Y was Rawcliffe's Scania 142E rated at 175 tons although it was only grossing about half that figure on this run. The weight is taken on a 1976 Dyson semi-trailer featuring water suspension and a self-tracking fourth axle.*

Above *Terry Thompson is at the wheel of DVN 313V heading down the A18 through the slush towards Immingham. Sitting on the Nicolas semi-trailer is a Belloit and Walmsley paper drying drum that Terry collected from the manufacturer on 11 January 1980. At 20-ft long and 59 tons in weight the drum was destined for delivery in Lilla Edet, Sweden. The self-steering axles on the trailer are shown to good accord although they seem to have offended the double white line.*

Below *When you have the right ship at the correct state of the tide then even loading record-breaking 401-ton vessels can seem fairly straightforward. Produced by GEC at Larne, these moisture separator reheaters were the last two of four vessels built for the San Onofre power station in California. Wrekin Roadways are seen during 1978 moving the last few inches off Northern Irish soil at Belfast docks on to the MV* Starman Australia.

Prior to the early 1970s this example of moving a fully-rigged drag line was a regular occurrence for, legally speaking, once the excessive jib was removed it had to be carried on a separate vehicle. The practical problem of negotiating a tight turn is surmounted by the Hope crew who demonstrate how to slew the crawler on the move. The AEC Mandator-Dyson low loader is taking the machine to West Drayton for work on the then new M4 project.

booms so when they were moved from site to site, the haulier had the choice of either leaving the boom on the machine or dismantling it into several pieces. As far as the law was concerned if the boom was removed it had to be carried on another vehicle so naturally the haulier, due to pressure from his cost-counting customer simply carried the machine as it stood along with its inbuilt 20- or 30-ft overhang. Fighting their way from site to site heavy haulage crews found they had to be experts in slewing the crane round whilst it was on the back of the low loader on the move as getting through places like Stamford was just impossible unless this technique was adopted.

The law might be considered an ass in some respects but after witnessing this type of lawful yet rather hazardous movement, in the early 1970s the legislators amended the Special Types Order to allow what they termed as 'constituent parts' to be removed from engineering plant to facilitate safer carriage and yet be carried on the same

Above *The S20 cabbed Foden was certainly aesthetically pleasing. These Ameys outfits are seen about to leave Tallington with Dow Mac beams destined for a footbridge in Havant, Hampshire. Not a great deal of power with only 150 bhp from its Gardner 6LX engine, the hauling Foden got most of its strength via the hand-operated reduction hubs on its back bogie being driven through the twelve-speed underdrive gearbox.*

Below *Dow Mac (Concrete) Ltd had two 6 × 4 tractors specially built for them by ERF fitted with high-power Cummins engines and 'beefed-up' specification brakes. The tractor, hauling a King bogie, is seen in 1969 about to deliver a 36-ton, 70-ft long beam which was used in the construction of the Coventry ring road. Sixteen years later the load-carrying King is still in regular use with Stillers, Darlington.*

Above *A. L. Crawford of Pippin Heath, Holt, Norfolk are not unusual in that a great deal of their traffic is concrete beams. What is quite rare is their use of this eight-wheeled bogie which started life originally with an engine and an ERF badge on its front, carrying sand, shingle and sugar beet for Lenny Allison of Sharrington. John Morley found the outfit in convoy waiting to unload its 55-ton load during the night at Middlesbrough in early July 1985.*

Below *One big asset that the tractor and bogie outfit has over the long-length artic is that once the load is removed the outfit reduces its size considerably as this photograph illustrates. Hope's unladen Mandator waits for the bigger Mammoth Major, grossing about 60 tons, to have its multi-load of Kingsbury beams removed to form part of the M5 under construction in Worcestershire.*

Above *Even though this 17-ton overhead travelling crane section was 115 ft in length, the AEC Mandator Mk V made easy work of the haul between Glasgow and Ruxley Corner, Sidcup, Kent, in about 1962. Resting on an American-made Timkin-axled bogie, the load was hauled the 435 mile route in only 24 hours.*

Below *One of the hazards of using a steerable bogie was demonstrated when this load of girders went out of control in North Road, Middlesbrough during 1975 because the locating pin did not find the required slot. Fortunately the only injury was to the roadside wall.*

Originally built by Rogers as a tank transporter, this trailer was converted by Simmons Engineering to the design of Hill of Botley. The 60-ton capacity unit is seen at Vosper Thornycroft's yard during 1968, moving this 56-ton load which had an 18 ft beam and 30 ft overall length within the yard. The pushing Scammell is MUH 21 which started life with Feltham Engineering of Middlesex.

vehicle. This was a major change in the regulations. Knowing that heavy hauliers were renowned for exploiting any loophole in the law, in bringing this amendment into force the law makers laid down strict conditions as to when and how it applied, which included a restriction of 75 tons gross weight and a strict legal definition of the term 'engineering plant'.

The only other major change to that 1931 Special Types Order was in allowing a practice which the hauliers had adopted, quite illegally, but which was accepted as being fairly reasonable and which probably started off in the area of carrying concrete beams. It often happened that when a contract was won for a new bridge or series of bridges to be built, then a large number of long beams had to be moved from places like Tallington near Stamford or Accrington in Lancashire. Rather than have, say, twenty long loads cluttering up the road all going to and from the same place, it seemed plain common sense to allow the heavy haulier to carry more than one beam so the number of loads were reduced. Once again the legis-

Above and opposite *Whilst Hallett Silbermann ably demonstrate how they carried this plane fuselage in Suffolk during 1966 (above), Hill of Botley show off their prowess by carrying the whole thing, albeit not on the public roads (opposite). Hill actually moved two of these Hawker Siddley 748s at Portsmouth Airport on 16 August 1967 after they had both crash landed in separate incidents. Robert Bernard was at the wheel of XMT 45 which hauled the plane across the airfield on an American step-frame trailer.*

lators laid down strict restrictions when more than one 'abnormal load' was being carried which included a gross weight limitation, once again of 75 tons.

Apart from being obliged to serve notices to people like the police and the Highway Authorities, the heavy haulier is given a great deal of freedom in how he moves these abnormal loads on the public roads. However once his dimensions exceed an overall width of 20 ft, a rigid length of 90 ft or a gross weight of 150 tons then movement is not permitted under the Special Types General Order and a specific order for the load or loads has to be obtained from the Department of Transport to cover its movement. There is also a restriction on loads between 14 ft 1 in and 20 ft wide for they require a VR1 authorization although in all other respects the General Order applies. These restrictions thus mean that the Department has the final say as to whether the really outsize loads go all the way by road or whether they have to be moved using a combination of road, rail or even sea transport. Some indication of how many loads this covers is illustrated by the fact that in 1976 the Department of Transport granted 319 Special Orders whereas in 1980 the figure was 238, although each order often included more than one movement. The majority of these moves relate to loads in excess of 90 ft long with less than ten per cent of those involved being vehicles specifically authorized because their gross weight was in excess of 150 tons.

The Department of Transport objectives of trying to reduce inconvenience to other road users and avoid road damage sometimes causes them to be accused of not being in support of the road transport industry although they do endeavour to be as fair as possible in their decisions. However one particular movement which took place in 1967 illustrates the difficulties that can be created. An engineering company based in Croydon had been commissioned to build a stainless-steel fractionating column for a new plant in Workington and intended that like all its other products, it should be delivered to site by road. With a weight of only 17 tons and width of 10 ft 3 in, this should not have created any problems, although its length of 100 ft 6 in meant that a special order had to be applied for to allow for the 300-mile journey by road. In response to the application the Department suggested that British Rail might be able to handle this vessel or that alternatively the manufacturers might care to consider transporting the column by sea from London Docks to Barrow in Furness. The engineers had already been quoted a price of £650 for the cross-country road haul and obviously this had been incorporated in the original price for the column of £16,000. To carry the load mainly by sea would have cost £6,537 whilst the rail-dominated version was nearly twice the price of the road move at £1,125. Even with this heavy costing difference the Department declined to authorize the all-road move and the job went to British Rail, although with separate road hauls at either end.

The discontent did not end there for unfortunately, when a British Rail inspector came to take details of the vessel, subsequent calculations showed that the column would have to be structurally

The Menai Bridge may have been freed from its toll restriction in 1940 but its narrow width still barred many loads from entering Anglesey. Wynn's are seen to make good use of a tilt frame to squeeze their way through with this car ferry ramp that they hauled from Chepstow to Holyhead using a double-drive Guy Invincible.

altered before it could be carried by rail. Neither the manufacturer nor their customer wanted the column to be altered so the Department was approached again hoping that they would change their mind due to this major hiccup. However they stuck to their guns and the vessel had to be modified. Not being able to do it themselves, British Rail sub-contracted the lifting and road movements at the start of the haul to a crane hire company who in turn sub-contracted the actual haulage to another operator. Due to the size of the load this haulier couldn't do it and another was eventually involved, but this was only two days before the move had to be performed meaning that thorough planning and route surveys had to be skimped. This stretching of the channels between the manufacturers and the people who were eventually going to do the road haulage nearly backfired altogether, for on the afternoon the load was due to move a road repair gang arrived and promptly dug a hole in the street making exit from the works impossible with a load of this length! They were eventually persuaded to hasten their work and the load did leave at 10 pm on the Friday night, being scheduled to arrive on site the following Wednesday. Had the haul been done completely by road it would have cost just half the price, taken two days less to perform and would not have required this expensive column to be structurally modified.

It should be stressed that incidents like this are few and far between and the Department of Transport feel they have a very good working relationship with the select heavy hauliers who move special order loads. Nevertheless there are still occasions when the haulier has to improvise to find a way round the regulations. The length and weight of a load may be difficult to alter but very good liaison between a heavy haulier and his customer will ensure that the manufacturer is very much aware of the legal problems that could be encountered before he sets to and builds his product. For instance it may be possible for an object to be made in two pieces which are joined up on site.

As far as reducing the width goes the heavy haulier has learnt a trick or two over the years, for now tilt frames are a standard piece of equipment in most yards. The principle is fairly simple—if you have a load which is just into VR1 width at, say, 15 ft, it may be that tilting it over at an angle, while not altering its physical dimensions, will alter the overall running width, which is measured on a horizontal plane between the two vertical extremities, considerably and by increasing the angle of tilt the width might be made to sneak under the 14 ft 1 in

Jimmy Wood and his Leeds-based Junior Constructor made page three of the Daily Express *with this Ashmore vessel in November 1958 but the only vital statistics it mentioned were the 45-ton weight, 122-ft length and 15-ft diameter, plus the length of the traffic queues it created in its struggle through Oldham and Manchester. It took seven foggy days to travel the 146 miles from Teesside to Birkenhead which reflects on the difficulties the load created. Destined for Ireland the load crossed the water in Bradwell fashion, towed by a tug.*

restriction. This concept of using either a fixed or variable tilt frame will obviously increase the running height but as far as the law is concerned there is no limit to the height of abnormal loads, for there seems no need for the law to create any restrictions when there are numerous physical ones, like bridges, barring progress to the unwary. These headaches can normally be surmounted with good planning but one vexatious problem which has hung round the neck of abnormal load carriers like an albatross is that of their speed limits.

In 1931 the clanking steamer pulling solid-tyred trailers that may or may not have had a coating of rubber, had a speed restriction of 5 mph imposed on it. This also applied to the new low-loading artics although if they were fitted with pneumatic tyres to the front steering axle then the limit was increased to 8 mph. In 1940 the un-rubber-covered wheel was outlawed totally and the speed limit was eventually increased to 12 mph. It was some considerable time ago that Roger Bannister became the first man to run a mile at an average speed of just over 15 mph but in 1985 vehicles carrying abnormal loads under the Authorization of Special Types General Order 1979 were still limited to 12 mph when travelling on any road other than a special road. This limit applied if your gross weight was 40 tons or 140 tons. Even unladen, whilst a normal haulage low loader could travel along a dual carriageway quite legally at 50 mph, a special types vehicle, which outwardly may look identical to its smaller capacity counterpart, was restricted to 20 mph.

These limits may sound hard to believe but the most difficult part to comprehend about the legislation is that although the Special Types Orders have always laid down speed restrictions, they have never created an offence of exceeding the speed limit given. The orders may have stated that you had to serve various notices on the relevant authorities before you moved your load, but if you didn't send them out you hadn't committed an offence of failing to serve the notices as no such offence existed. In fact there were never any offences at all from any of the various Special Types Orders enacted since 1931 for all these orders did was to specifically authorize, by ministerial approval, the use of certain vehicles on the road. The minister laid down certain conditions to meet his approval (like service of notices and speed limits) so if you didn't conform to his conditions then his approval was withdrawn and your vehicle was considered to come under regulations that governed every other goods vehicle on the road. Therefore if a vehicle was driven at say 30 mph, not on a special road, the driver was not committing an offence of exceeding the 12 mph limit, but the driver and his company were committing offences

Above and below *The method and criteria adopted in the escorting of abnormal loads varies considerably amongst differing police forces. The Zephyr Six escorting the Hallett-supported Canberra bomber wings is relying on a written message to warn other motorists. Cleveland Police prefer to have their escorting officers on manoeuvrable motor cycles, PC Smith and PC Grievson are seen by Mick Fountain with this 120-ton gross Econofreight outfit en route from Billingham to Wilton, in April 1981.*

Above *It has been known for the supervising police to get it wrong! Anthony Blake of Richmond was on hand to record this embarrassing moment when the escort got lost and took the Sunter crew off their scheduled route. The 18-ft 3-in wide fabrication was part of a wave-making machine destined for Portsmouth. JAJ 496 was a 6 × 4 Mammoth Major and was the first new vehicle bought by the Sunter Brothers following denationalization. It was being used on contract licence to Head Wrightson.*

Below *The police escort may not please everybody but without them the heavy haulier would have great difficulty in moving loads, especially if they are like these two monsters seen by Tony Storry on the A19 at Middlesbrough on 21 July 1985. At 35-ft wide, these ITM-Head Wrightson dock gates were the widest loads to traverse Cleveland when they were hauled from Thornaby to Normanby Wharf. Ken Bickerton is the leading driver, his charge partially obscuring Bill Jamieson in LAJ 798P. The all-up weight of the individual Contractor-Nicolas outfits is only 156.3 tons. The tasks of the Sunter men are being orchestrated by Jack Higgins who is keeping in radio communication from the leading Scammell's running board.*

of excess weight, trailer too wide, outfit too long etc. From being exempted from certain regulations, non-compliance with the Special Types Orders removed the protection they afforded and made those involved liable for all the offences in the book. Over the years, heavy hauliers gradually accepted this odd idiosyncracy in the law but it was probably the introduction of the tachograph that brought things to a head. Speeding is an offence which by law requires corroboration therefore the mere fact that there is a speed trace on a tachograph disc which shows that the limit was exceeded does not make the driver liable to be prosecuted for speeding. However certain enforcement agencies used this disc as evidence to show that the vehicle was not being operated as per the Special Types Order therefore charges of excess weight were preferred.

Some people may not be aware that as well as the police, haulage contractors have several other agencies overseeing their operations who can prefer charges and take them to court. However people like the Trading Standard Officers did come into conflict with the police over this speed trace for the latter are the only agency who escort abnormal loads on the road. Police forces throughout the country may vary in the criteria of when and how loads are escorted but when considering what speed the load should travel at, it is safety, not the speed limit which will come to the fore. Thus to ease congestion loads may travel far faster than the 12 mph limit although with bigger loads even 5 mph may be the maximum. The police escort rarely satisfies every other road user in the vicinity of an abnormal load but without him the heavy haulier would have much more difficulty in doing his job of moving loads from A to B.

However, as 1986 progresses, the sanity of new legislation is a bright glimmer on the horizon. Complicated rules will still apply, but a refreshing attitude towards the speed of vehicles is being traded for tighter controls on the vehicles themselves and the number of axles in use.

Chapter 4

Getting from A to B

On Sunday 25 March 1984 Sunters were involved in the movement of quite a load. At 303 tons in weight it wasn't the heaviest load they had ever moved and at 24 ft 8 in broad it was not the widest but at 221 ft 2 in in length it was at the time the longest load ever to be moved on roads in this country. The absorption column was a major part of a new nitric acid plant being built in ICI Billingham and was constructed by the long-established heavy engineering company of Head Wrightson (Teesdale) Ltd, Thornaby. From their heyday of the 1950s and 60s, Head Wrightson's business had slowly declined due to lack of orders. Following the building of this longest load their parent

During July/August 1947 Pickfords delivered this 45,000-KVA C. A. Parson transformer into CEB Nursling. It was only a short road haul up the Romsey road from Millbrook Station, Southampton, but some indication of the difficulty the crew had is reflected in how the hauling Diamond T tractor had to turn the Crane trailer. The round plates on the roadway were necessary because of the soft surface.

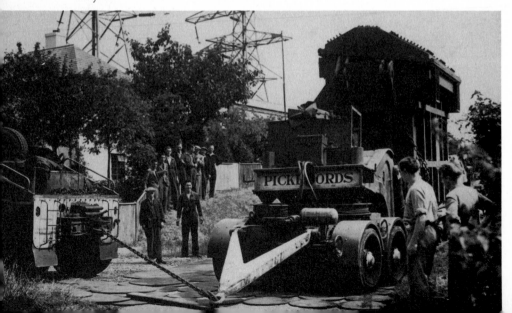

It would still be quite a haul in the 1980s, but when Siddle Cook's MPT 527 moved this 150-ft long, 10-ft diameter splitter column in February 1956 it created quite a stir down the length of England. With inferior equipment and a poor road layout it was a marvel that they managed to move the 51-ton load from Newcastle to Shellhaven. Things look tight in this Newcastle Chronicle *photograph taken at North Heaton, but the highlight of the nine-day move was spending an hour getting round Gants Hill roundabout at Ilford.*

company of Davey sold them to the locally-based international consortium of ITM who were able to keep them going in the manufacturing field.

The problems of Head Wrightson were well known to the local community who as individuals were virtually powerless to control their plight. What they did do when this massive load crossed Teesside at an average speed of 1 mph was to come and stand, watch and admire its slow controlled passage. Some walked the 6 miles alongside the Sunter crew but nearly all would be wondering if Head Wrightson would survive beyond the next few months. The local television sent a crew out to record the movement whilst a local radio station revolved its Sunday morning programme around the load with a radio car keeping one step ahead. The load made a carnival occasion on a bright but cool day and although the crew had enough problems with adverse cambers, never mind the numerous photographers leaping out, their expertise meant the move passed off without incident.

Contrast this exciting occasion to events nearly thirty years earlier. Annis moved a 35-ton bubble chamber from Harwell to Southampton after it had been on loan from French atomic scientists for important research work. With a height of 21 ft 6 in and width of 18 ft it meant that instead of driving the 55 miles straight down the A34, the Annis crew had to travel nearly four times that distance to safely deliver the load to the docks. A telephone wire was broken at Brack-

Above left *During August 1951, Joe Stainthorpe of Pickford's Birtley depot supervised the move of this Ransome & Rapier W90 excavator base in one piece between open cast sites in County Durham. The machine was first walked over a specially-prepared trench and after removing the tracks it was jacked down on to the Crane 32-wheeler. At 25-ft wide and 95 tons in weight it was quite a load for the day and although 30 yd of hedge had to be removed the valuable machine was only out of commission for fourteen days rather than the three months required if the conventional method of totally stripping the machine had been adopted.*

Above right *Hill of Botley are seen in 1962 demonstrating how invaluable a slow-pulling winch can be in ensuring that bridges can be crossed without the necessity of a heavy hauling tractor. Titch Nutley is walking beside the 90-ton Crane girder trailer carrying a 54 RB excavator, en route from Trawsfynydd reservoir to Blaenau Ffestiniog in North Wales.*

Below *At 40-ft wide and 30-ft high, this bow section may have been quite a problem had it been routed down Sauchiehall Street but fortunately for Pickfords' Glasgow manager Alec MacKinlay, all he had to worry about was the unevenness of Alexander Stephen and Sons' shipyard at Linthouse. Supported on a 110-ton capacity Crane trailer, the 43.46-ton load took a couple of hours to travel the one mile between the fabricating bay and the building berth where it formed the top bow unit of a 10,000-ton refrigerating ship being built for the Port Line.*

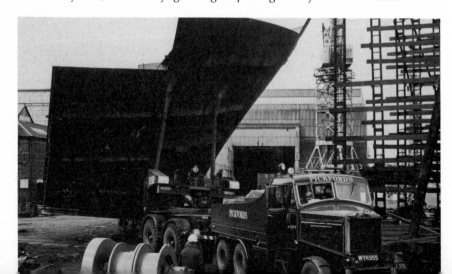

nell and a school sign post had to be bent out of the way at Woking-
ham. Apart from this only a few small tree branches and leaves were
brought down by the high load but the movement prompted one
reporter to write of 'trails of chaos and destruction' being caused by
the load.

When Siddle Cooks moved a 51-ton, 127-ft long steel column from
Newcastle to London in early 1956 banner headlines read 'One for the
road? Not if it's a load of this size.' The article was a damning swathe
against road-going heavy haulage. It charged the industry with
causing endless delay, congestion and general frustration to other
road users plus exacting a heavy toll in damaged telegraph poles,
lamp standards and traffic signs most of which had to be made good
at public expense. It stated that it tied up the services of hundreds of
police who could have been employed more profitably on other jobs.
The feature as a whole made the supporters of heavy haulage wince
but inside it was a germ of truth. 'Our present road system is utterly
and absolutely inadequate, not to say dangerous in some cases' was
how E. E. Smith put it and to find fault with this remark would have
taken some justifying. The problem was that whilst ever-increasing
demands were being made on heavy hauliers during the 1950s to
move bigger and heavier weights, both the equipment they were
using and the roads they had to go along were not keeping abreast
with their traffic. Thirty years on both equipment and roads have
improved dramatically, the demise now being in the manufacturers
who build these massive loads forcing established heavy haulage
names like Pickfords and Wynns to tighten their belts and driving
others like Watkinsons of Keighley completely out of business. This
change round in fortunes has not gone unnoticed— lots of people
now seem to treat the sight of a massive load trundling down the road
as part of a rare breed which should really be encouraged, especially
when it is hauling a home-produced load. Being able to deliver the
goods is where the expertise of the heavy haulier can be seen to shine
with those who have managed to weather the passage of time
collecting lots of know-how in getting their load exactly from the
place where it is to where it is required.

The eighteen months following May 1958 found Sunters involved
in the movement of twelve heat exchangers which originated from
Head Wrightson of Thornaby and were delivered to the then new
power station being built at Bradwell in Essex. Each of these 238-ton
monsters only travelled 1½ miles on the road because the majority of
the journey was spent surrounded by salt water as they were towed
majestically down the North Sea. This concept of delivery may have

When asked to test this Swedish Lloyd ferry slipway at Southampton in 1962, Hill of Botley placed 300 tons of ballast on to three of their assorted trailers and moved them about using a 6 × 6 Rolls-Royce-powered Super Constructor. Redpath, Dorman and Long may have guaranteed compensation to Hill if the outfits slipped into the sea, but it was a worrying time for the Hill men. 358 ETN had started life in Northumberland as a drilling rig but after being burnt out it was bought by Hill and converted for heavy haulage use.

been new to Sunters but Head Wrightson had used it quite often to deliver dock gates without cluttering up the road. A couple of years later they delivered four 26-ft diameter boilers to Dungeness but because the beach affronting the power station was shingle to a depth of 60 ft, they could not follow the same method as they used in Essex of building a concrete pad down into the water. On this occasion two winches pulled these 430-ton masses straight from the sea and simply bowled them up the foreshore to firmer ground. Working through a system of six pulley blocks, the effort had to be well orchestrated as the boilers were rolled on to a specially-built railway truck which in turn was pulled with little fuss straight into the intended heart of the power station.

In September 1966 Sunters were again working with Head Wrightson to deliver another vessel just down the river from Thornaby to the Oil Refinery being built for Shell at Teesport. With only one column to move it was decided to press into use an old World

War 2 slipway rather than build an expensive new one. A dredger was used to ensure that the 22-ft diameter vessel had ample clearance but all this succeeded in doing was to dredge away half the slipway! This was rebuilt but it still sweated hard under the 90 tons thrown on to the solid-tyred back bogie as the vessel eased down on to it when the tide receded. With a length of 148 ft it meant this back bogie was pushed well into the river and with less than two hours elapsing between the wheels appearing and disappearing again under the incoming tide, it meant that rear steerman Dessy Gibson was up to his knees for an early bath as the load was inched back on to dry land.

Sunters weren't the only haulier to be involved with a waterborne method of delivery for the idea, especially with more traditional nautical types of load, was well established in history. As early as June 1931 a large Ruth's steam accumulator was slipped into the River Annan and towed via the Solway Firth and the Firth of Clyde, being pulled out of the water just outside Greenock. Two Burrells and a McLaren road locomotive were the traction provided by Road Engines and Kerr who finished the journey off into the Westburn Sugar Refinery using a steel-wheel shod trailer that was steered by splitting the drawbar in half.

Pickfords too have used this method, for in 1955 they moved a 140-ft-long, 14-ft-diameter, 85-ton distillation column manufactured by G. & A. Harvey of London and destined for Forth Chemicals Ltd at Grangemouth. The journey from Thames to Forth was undertaken along the North Sea. Pickfords adopted a different method to get the column back on to the solid-tyred road-going bogies. They utilized three Scammell Pioneer 80-ton tractor-based winches to simply rotate the vessel about its length, up a crude ramp out of the water and gently on to the strategically-placed bogies.

Scotland may certainly have more than its share of fine roaming countryside but one thing it lacks is a variety of strong roads. Even in 1985 any load heavier than 150 tons just could not be hauled by road from Glasgow to Edinburgh or vice versa because there just wasn't a route strong enough to take it. The cross-country journey of no more than 50 miles was therefore replaced by a long costly sea passage which covered nearly all the coast line of Scotland.

At times, however, weight limits go out the window, after due consideration with the relevant authorities, as Pickfords then Scottish Manager Alec McKinlay found when they were asked to move three loads into the Nant Generating Station in the heart of Argyllshire. With the stator, rotor and transformer only weighing in at 40 tons, 35 tons and 60 tons respectively it didn't seem that difficult a job but

Top, above and below *During 1955 Pickfords delivered this 85-ton distillation column from its manufacturers G. & A. Harvey Ltd to Forth Chemicals at Grangemouth. The leg between the Thames and the Firth of Forth saw the 140-ft long, 14-ft diameter vessel towed behind a sea-going tug. Here it is seen being winched on to the Crane bogies near Kinneil on the outskirts of Bo'ness in a particularly interesting fashion more seen in traditional forestry work.*

Above *Bill Jamieson is at the helm of 447 DPY as the Sunter Scammell is about to ease one of the eight Whessoe stainless steel vessels built in Stockton and taken to Ringaskiddy, Southern Ireland during 1971. The sea-going mount is a pair of Rhine barges lashed together, their shallow draught and beaching ability meant the eventual road haul was kept to a minimum.*

Right *Some heavy haulage drivers say that the back roads of Scotland are built on bogs. This photograph tends to support their line of thought.*

Lundin Road is one of the many places etched in the memory of any heavy haulage crews that have travelled from Rosyth into Kincardine Power Station, Fife. Even with DUS 951 pulling alongside TGJ 681, the incline and turn still prevented progress. An extra 6 × 6 Constructor in the guise of M1457 SUU 263, plus the old 80-tonner pushing at the rear, eventually prompted forward movement resulting in another load safely delivered.

when you realize that the last 11 miles of the haul were on roads which normally carried a 12-ton weight limit, it reflects on the terrain that was involved. Selecting a suitable trailer wasn't that difficult for the new sophisticated girder trailers on pneumatics had to be excluded because of their cumbersome length and width. The old Crane 32-wheeler on solid tyres, which comprised two sixteen-wheeled bogies joined together by a short table top, offered a very short load carrier with all-wheel steering but even at 9 ft wide it was still a foot wider than some of the stretches of road it was to travel on. It was also fairly heavy and all-up weight with the two pull/push Scammells hauling the heaviest of the three loads was over ten times that 12-ton restriction.

Leaving the A85 at Taynuilt, the outfit headed up Glen Nant towards Kilchrenan but forward momentum was regularly stopped to lay steel plates over the roadway, not only because of weak bridges and culverts but also because the main GPO Transatlantic telephone cable ran under the road at numerous places and breaking that would have been too costly even to think about. At Kilchrenan the route turned right on to a track more suitable for mountain goats. The leading Constructor was losing diesel from its fuel tank due to the angle of inclination that it had to be driven at. There was no chance of stopping either for the Crane trailer seemed to adopt a half-sunken posture on parts of the sponge-like road so the crawling speed had to be maintained at all costs. The generating station was eventually reached although the last 10 miles took over 11 hours to complete.

Scottish folk have come to accept that there may be some short-comings in their road network but when the cause is good enough a way can always be found round an impossibility. Siddle Cook's RPT 400, a standard Scammell 25-tonner, found itself in the village of Tomintoul, Banffshire one day although how it actually got there still seems incredible. The road from Grantown-on-Spey to Ballater may have an A classification but some of the inclines on it are so steep that it can be first-gear work even for a car, never mind a Gardner 6LW-powered artic. The Cook outfit had only managed to reach the village after being double headed by a farm tractor to sledge itself over two acute river bridges, but once at Tomintoul the problem wasn't the Scammell's lack of power or its gross weight, but that its 55-ft length just wouldn't permit it to turn left on the Dufftown road without knocking down a couple of houses. True the driver should have really followed a different route altogether to get to Tomnavoulin but now he couldn't even turn round never mind consider retracing his steps so the problem of turning left just had to be surmounted.

After walking round on foot the crew discovered that if they

Built in Schiedam, Holland, and destined for the BP refinery Llandarcy at Neath, Glamorgan, this 26-ft diameter pressure vessel was transported in two halves. There may have only been 46 tons in each of these loads but Wynn's Contractor-Crane outfits preferred to cut this corner rather than risk the cross fall on the conventional right turn.

reversed slightly away from the corner then by turning off behind some shops they could make the Dufftown road by driving across a field of rough pasture. With permission granted by the owners and the local constable giving directions, the Scammell pushed down the wire fence and managed to return to its prescribed route well beyond the offending corner. The fence was replaced and Tomintoul waved farewell to that long step-frame artic from Consett. The earth-moving equipment it was carrying was required in the construction of a new whisky distillery so it was well worth the village having to undergo some minor cosmetic modifications!

Fred Hope tells another story of how a corner was turned in Scotland but this one seems rather too long in both senses of the word. Hope had won a contract to move a considerable number of 100 ft long Oregon pine trees and with so many loads to deliver it meant that not every driver who was used had as much experience as the others on long-load work. Steerable rear bogies were not in great abundance either and when one particular load got stuck, Fred said that the only way the driver could extricate himself from the predicament was to go to the Town Hall and ask there if they could kindly open the large front doors so that the load of trees could be reversed in to allow him to negotiate the corner!

The problems of the basic road pattern can normally be surmounted by plating over or short cutting an obstruction but it is the man-made obstructions like bridges that normally cause the biggest of headaches, especially if they belong to another interested party like the railways or the canal authorities. Being on the go longer than most Pickfords have learnt quite a lot about bridges and have the infamous reputation of having had two different bridges totally collapse on them. The attitude they have adopted in getting under them

Opposite top *At 135 tons in weight this demethanizer column was one of two similar loads that Pickfords were obliged to squeeze under a 14 ft railbridge en route from Fraserburgh harbour to St Fergus during November 1978 and February 1979. Even using the mature low-slung Crane solid-tyred bogies the height was still restrictive but with the use of a pair of heavy duty skates and a plated roadway, Pickfords made the obstacle seem insignificant.*

Opposite middle and bottom *Wynn's have also shown that whilst a low bridge may be a slight impediment it is rarely a total barrier to the ingenious heavy haulier. The photographs demonstrate how they managed to get this Whessoe pressure vessel to its eventual destination at a gas works in Cardiff during 1961. They were assisted by a plate of steel, Coles and Lorraine craneage plus a representative of the law.*

has varied according to the type of load that they have carried. In 1936 they hauled an 80-ton armature to a South Wales steel works and on the face of it they just couldn't have got this load under a particular restrictive bridge. What they did was to simply dig down underneath this railway bridge so the eventual head height was increased enough to let them squeeze under.

Less expensive but just as efficient was the method used when Pickfords hauled two 128 ft long demethanizer columns from Fraserburgh to the gas extraction plant at St Fergus in late 1978 and early 1979. At that time the only route available took them under a rail bridge offering only 14 ft 3 in clearance. The 135-ton columns were 12 ft 8 in in diameter at their biggest end so even using a pair of the old Crane solid-tyred bogies, which are far lower than the modern-day hydraulic modular bogies, they would have still been too high. What Pickfords did here was to stop at the bridge, lift the one offending end of the load off the leading bogie by crane and rest it on two large skates which are normally pressed into use when the big girder trailers are being separated. The hauling Scammell then drove under the bridge and winched the load through, the smaller end of the column being able to sneak under without being disturbed from its carrying bogie. Lifting the load back on to the carrier proper at the other side of the bridge again by crane meant the haul could be finished in the normal fashion.

Siddle Cooks have rolled loads under bridges and reloaded at the other side but a more refined method was demonstrated by Wynns when they were delivering a series of Whessoe pressure vessels from Darlington to Cardiff in 1961. Like most heavy hauls where the greatest difficulty of the job can often be encountered either at the point of departure or just about the point of delivery, these moves were no exception. There was no alternative but to squeeze under a 13-ft 3-in bridge which gave direct access to the gas works which was awaiting delivery of the 30-ton loads. With a running height of 15 ft 8 in it meant that a great deal of space had to be gained from somewhere but Wynns solved the problem by first using their own craneage to unload the vessel from the trailer and lay it on a large steel plate. The hauling Diamond T then dragged the plate and the load under the bridge with ample clearance where the cranes restored it to the smoother running Scheuerle load carrier. One of these vessels had already got stuck under a 15-ft 9-in bridge on Whitehall Road at Leeds as the road surface had crept upwards due to resurfacing with the passage of time. The load was extricated on this occasion by simply

Above *For the four years after 1956, following the closing of the A40 road bridge over the River Severn at Gloucester, loads in excess of 90 tons destined for South Wales were obliged to take an odd diversion. To cross the water the loads had to be transhipped on to a suitable rail truck for the 400-yd stretch between the Gloucester railway siding and 'The Dog' siding further down the line. This photograph shows the Wynn's crew at work skidding the mill housing sideways. Wynn's fleet number 202, in the background, is a Ward Le France wrecker registration number EDW 340.*

Below *Heavy haulage is a business of life-long experience that cannot and will not be rushed. It demands more than its fair share of the highway and it dictates the use of it at its own measured pace. The general motoring public tends to forget that there may have been three Cummins-powered Pacifics clawing their way upward, but at less than 2 bhp per ton all up weight, hill restarts are a situation too frightening even to contemplate.*

Above *PUC 472 is seen in Wincomblee Road, Newcastle, negotiating a Pickfords-manufactured ramp required to ease the vicious cross fall as the 120-ton Parson transformer makes its way towards the Vickers Naval yard. Destined eventually for delivery in Carlisle, the load was shipped by sea from the Tyne to Liverpool and thence up the west coast as there was no suitable direct cross-country route for a load of this size.*

Below and opposite *The gateway of Distington Engineering at Workington (below) has been an impressive backdrop to many large loads that have left the works, but unfortunately when the company produced this abnormal funnel (opposite) it may have been light enough for an Octopus but it was embarrassingly too wide to leave the premises. The problem was eventually solved by craning the load over the wall and reloading the BRS vehicle at the other side.*

letting down some of the many tyres on the 32-wheeled trailer.

Wynns had been obliged to weather the years between 1956 and 1960 through plain hard work for every time they had brought a load in excess of 90 tons to Gloucester and destined for South Wales, their traffic had taken an odd diversion. For the four years prior to the Ross Spur opening there wasn't a suitable bridge strong enough to take this weight over the River Severn. Loads which were too big to go by rail all the way were brought to Gloucester railway station by Wynns, and transferred to special railway trucks. They were hauled the 400 yd over the railway river bridge then loaded back on to the Wynns outfit at the other side. With no suitable craneage available at either point, the loads had to be moved across in the traditional side-skidding manner.

Pickfords had to adopt a similar procedure when they were delivering a 125-ton Babcock boiler to a plant at Workington in 1979. There was no way the 25-ft-high load would go under the bridge so 600 yd of the latter part of the journey was done by means of rail. In this particular case there was a suitable route into the factory from the other direction which would have avoided this low bridge, however when Pickfords applied for this route on their special order it was refused. They were told that this way would have taken them past an historic yew tree and conservationists would not tolerate the slightest possibility that any damage could be caused to

Above and below *Prior to building a new generation of electrical equipment, C. A. Parsons were obliged to install 300-ton capacity craneage. The girders were built by Clyde, Crane & Booth Ltd of Mossend and Rodley. The haul to Newcastle was hit badly by inclement weather and as these photographs show the McKelvie crew had their work cut out to get their 105-ft long loads into the required position inside the works by 5 March 1963.*

overhanging branches.

When new roads are built construction engineers have the chance to iron out a black spot or two, although things don't always go to plan. It wasn't a bridge that was the problem for traffic travelling south on the A595 from Egremont to BNFL's Sellafield plant, but a vicious downhill right turn on adverse camber at Calder Bridge caused a headache for the heavy haulier. It also created a great deal of congestion for cars at peak times so both problems should have been remedied when a new road was built to the site which missed out this picturesque village entirely. Chris Millers of Preston were pleased for they were the first to try out the route when they hauled two 54-ton storage vessels in convoy to the plant early in 1985. The stainless steel vessels, which were built in Thetford, Norfolk, were 49 ft long and 17 ft in diameter. They were routed first to Felixstowe and then by ship round the coast to Workington, but snow in great abundance haunted the Millers men on the first leg of the journey. Days were spent lost in snow drifts just jumping from one big lay-by to the next and even the sea leg of the journey was affected by bad weather. Rolling off into Cumbria Millers' Mack and Volvo made good progress right up to Hensingham where, of all things, the backing plate off the set of traffic lights stopped them from crossing The Square. Three men hauling on one rope soon remedied this obstruction and the haul was recommenced although when they reached the new road to Sellafield, the two big artics didn't take it. When this new stretch of road had been constructed a bridge had been built over it so these loads were obliged to go down into Calder Bridge after all. Rather than risk the right turn however, Millers preferred to drive past the corner, do a multi-point manoeuvre across the village centre car park, then approach the junction from the other direction which made it far easier to negotiate.

Even the standard motorway bridge can be a barrier to many heavy loads as it offers a clearance of only 16 ft 6 in so if you can't get below that your route from, say, London to Birmingham up the M1 is replaced by a considerably lengthened trek on one of the high-load routes which criss-cross the countryside. Chris Millers found that by investing in a new low-slung small-tyred semi-trailer particularly for the movement of fairly light brewery fermenting tanks, they were able to move a load per day on a particular job by using the M1 as part of their route. In contrast another more famous haulier was taking three days because his conventional load carrier had to travel on the high-load route. A matter of inches difference in the running height can be very critical indeed.

Lowering the running height to its minimum can be achieved of

Top *The trend to make our roadways more picturesque by planting trees along narrow central reservations may have its merits but as this Evesham Journal photograph suggests it is not without its drawbacks either. The Hallett Silbermann Foden has not got a great deal of weight in this packing case but its dimensions create their own problems.*

Bottom *At 135-ft long, this 35-ton crane girder was quite a testing load to move from Adamson Alliance at Telford to Round Oak steel works at Brierley Hill in 1975, especially as the route took the Contractor-Crane-bogied outfit right through the town centre of Dudley. Driver Dennis Roderick was quite a character who found little difficulty with this type of work. His own odd idiosyncrasy was to move his cap around as he was manoeuvring a big load so that whichever way his peak was pointing, this was his intended direction of travel.*

Top *It seems hard to understand how excessively long columns were moved before the arrival of the modular bogie concept. This photograph taken in October 1980 shows just how impressive this type of load can be. Described as being first wash, rectifier and drying columns, they were built by Head Wrightson for BP's number three ethanol plant in Grangemouth.*

Middle *A 90-ton payload is certainly heavy for some but as Wynn's Renown is probably the biggest articulated outfit in the land, moving this bottle sterilizing machine from Gomersal to Accrington during 1983 was fairly routine. Driver Len Dobie was assisted by Joe Pickton and Charlie Turner. This photograph illustrates how low wires may be rarely noticed by the car-driving public, but are a major concern to the reputable heavy haulier.*

Bottom *During early 1985, Wynn's Heavy Haulage delivered two 175-ton transformers from GEC at Stafford to Padiham power station in Lancashire. Leading driver Alan Williams and steersman Tom Gregory found themselves routed via the M6 and then the A59 towards Whalley. With motorway bridge heights being so critical, this photograph illustrates that at times the ex-Wrekin trailer WR50 was lowered off till it virtually scraped along the ground. It also used up most of the roadway.*

Above *Many heavy hauliers have moved parts of oil rigs, but Geoff Johnson's driver Bob Cook moved the complete thing on 9 September 1984, albeit in a slightly scaled-down version. Only 20 tons in weight but 22-ft wide and 21-ft high, the move from Teesside to Aycliffe did ruffle slightly the normal Sunday morning calm.*

Below *The girder trailer outfit has normally offered a variable width to suit different loads or in this case just to ease unladen running. This particular outfit just leaving Dereham was part of a big export success both for Scammell in selling their Contractors but mainly for Crane Fruehauf in being able to convince the USSR that their product rated for 350 tons payload could withstand the rigours of the extreme Russian climate.*

Above *On 24th April 1979 NAJ 103P pushed this Nicolas bogie back on to the Starman vessel moored in Teesport. The absorbtion column it is loading had been welded to the deck during transit but to allow the bogies to slip underneath, the crew lifted the mass 6 ft off the ground. The ship seems to be riding high in relation to the quay although the ramp does allow the hydraulic trailer to show off its level-riding characteristics but it is seen to be slightly arched in preparation for taking the weight.*

Below *Heavy haulage is a demanding profession and although the engineering plant type of load is probably the most regular cargoe carried it still demands the greatest of care in how you carry it and by which route you travel!*

Above *The column had a length of 193 ft and a diameter of 23 ft but it was the weight which proved the most awkward to handle, not so much because it was 257 tons but mainly because 180 tons of this was through the rearmost bogie, thus the need for a big imbalance in axle structure. Destined for ICI Wilton, the column took the normal high-load route via the private works of British Steel. YVN 308T has hooked itself on to the rear, the lengthy drawbar being used as a means of braking on the 1 in 13 descent.*

Below *It was not the longest haul done by Sunters but moving this accommodation unit at Glasgow on 5 November 1985 meant that the Northallerton haulier smashed the heaviest load moved by road record by a long way. The load weighed all of 1,305 tons, and with a width of 106 ft it meant that an extra road had to be laid down parallel to the original highway. The Tractomas and Titan are actually pushing the 55 foot high load backwards whilst on the other side are a pulling Volvo and another Titan in forward gear. It was a memorable day also for eleven-year-old Paul Campbell as Jimmy Saville had 'fixed it' so that he took the wheel of the Tractomas for a while during the site part of the move.*

Don Sutherland from the engineering company of Huwood recorded this end-suspension movement during 1967. Driver Billy Gilligan is assisted by Brian Hannah in Siddle C. Cook's Junior Constructor about to leave the Ellis works at Swalwell. The 30-ton load is supported on Crane bogies, their hydraulic suspension would make optimum use of the 18-in ground clearance on the haul to Seal Sands on Teesside.

course if the load is carried by means of end suspension, in other words if it is supported at its extremities by book ends. With no form of other support down its entire length it means that the concept isn't really suitable for any load which may be slightly weak or perhaps susceptible to damage, and of course the book ends must also be of sufficient strength to take this high loading. Ample strength can usually be guaranteed although ample space is sometimes a big problem. The question of whether a load will get through a particular bottle-neck or not can be answered if a dry run is performed, but to ensure the test is realistic enough then the dummy load must meet the same criterion which causes concern be it weight, width or length.

Rather than risk having a massive column sink through the road surface inside a private works at Stanlow, Econofreight Heavy Haulage loaded their trailers up with 200 tons of crane ballast and tested its strength the hard way. Econofreight also took a wide wooden box through the Tyne Tunnel to see if a similar dimensioned steel fabrication could make it but perhaps a more-witnessed test was performed on Sunday 30 November 1969.

The Central Electricity Generating Board were wanting to place a 162-ton transformer at the Indian Queens sub-station which is situated approximately 10 miles south of Bodmin on the A30. With no direct route available into Cornwall with a load of this weight from the north, it meant that a sea journey would have to precede the final

George Woller has moved many a mountainous load in his time with Pickfords, but this wooden framework must have been one of the most difficult. The flimsy construction simulated the dimensions of a transformer destined for the Indian Queen sub-station although all the CEGB were concerned about was whether the 131-ft long, 15-ft wide girder trailer outfit could squeeze itself through the narrow streets of Penzance. On Sunday 30 November 1969 George and his Scammell proved it could be done whilst just a few bystanders witnessed this memorable dry run!

stretch by road. Only Penzance was suitable for a start point, the geographically closer St Austell and Newquay both being impractical for other reasons. The 40-mile ride up the A30 may have been difficult enough but the CEGB's main concern was whether the 131-ft-long, 15-ft-wide girder-trailer outfit could physically squeeze itself through the narrow streets of Penzance. Pickfords were satisfied they could do it but the CEGB asked if they could prove it so on Saturday 29 November 1969, George Wooler driving Scammell Contractor NYE 594E rolled off the *Kingsnorth Fisher* on to the dockside at Penzance ready to show how bendable his outfit really was. At the time George already had 30 years of assorted experience with Pickfords but the wooden framework that was placed on to the twelve-axle Crane Fruehauf trailer must have been the lightest load he had ever carried.

Naturally most of the town came out to witness the sight of the Pickfords' road train creeping past. Down Promenade Road the Scammell turned right into Alexandra Road and although the next right into Alverton Road was acute, it still didn't bother John Hagan

When it came to actually move the load through Penzance, it was Wynn's who won the contract for the job. The shot suggests an ample amount of space around the Crane girder trailer although the Welsh crew did not break any speed records as they inched past the Market House at a measured rate. The ducting lying on top of the trailer is for later use with the air cushion equipment.

and Cyril Moulton, the Manchester-based trailermen. The crowds thickened up for they knew as the Scammell neared the Market Place that this was to be the tightest spot of all. The drama heightened as the road train, already moving at a snail's pace, was forever stopping as it went round the S bend. Someone shouted it that it was getting stuck but Pickfords Bristol depot manager Mr F. J. K. Wood, who was in charge of the operation, confirmed that the stop/starts were merely to allow measurements to be taken at the vital points.

George and his Scammell made it through the town although prior to retracing his steps the girder trailer was nipped in to a width of 11 ft 5 in, making the return journey an anti-climax. It was perhaps slightly ironical however that when it came to move the actual transformer in 1972, it was Wynns who did the job, albeit with an identical Scammell Contractor/Crane Fruehauf outfit. Both Pickfords and Wynns agree that were it not for the all-wheel manoeuvrability of the trailer then perhaps they wouldn't have cleared Penzance. Both companies are aware that it is only the dramatic improvement in equipment that makes the heavy haulier able to carry increasingly bigger and heavier loads.

Chapter 5

Progress onward

Over the last thirty years the heavy haulage world has witnessed a big change in the size of loads that are expected to be moved. Unlike the normal unanswerable question of which came first, the chicken or the egg, in the heavy transport game it was unquestionably the loads which were built first, the equipment to carry them satisfactorily gradually evolving as the need arose. In the main abnormal indivisible loads fall into two distinct classifications; those that can be carried resting on one trailer or semi-trailer and those that due to their size need to be supported on more than one vehicle or trailer.

The girder trailer is undoubtedly the strongest single unit on the roads today, its concept dating back to the realization that a trailer could be more adaptable, for heavy haulage work anyway, if the flooring was removed. Engineers like J. Hickey and Sons of London

Affectionately known as 'The Abortion', Pickfords' T3440 was a Crane sixteen-wheeler offering a capacity of 140 tons on its sturdy frame. The innovative jacking rams are clearly on show, these being the forerunners to the modern-day hydraulic suspension. The outfit is heading for Newcastle quayside in July 1951, the C. A. Parson load being destined for Ontario, Canada.

This page and top right
Technically speaking the crawler type of crane could be classed as being mobile, its wider tracks giving far better stability on site working conditions. Rigged for work there would be more than 100 tons sat in this Lima model (correctly named Baldwin Lima Hamilton of Ohio) but the problems of heavy lift work are not exaggerated in the launch of this luxury cruiser into the River Medway in Kent.

Middle right *Not so very long ago mobile craneage was normally the domain of the specialist heavy haulier, the limited lifting mechanisms being based on commercial vehicle chassis. Wynn's fleet number 207 was a Thornycroft Amazon, registration number FDW 752, a short 6 × 4 unit supporting a Coles crane. The outfit is pictured in South Wales unloading 125, a Bedford-Scammell artic incorporated into the Wynn's fleet in June 1945.*

Bottom right *TM1277 was one of the last generation of the big Crane Fruehauf girder trailers offering a capacity of 300 tons and an ability to drop its frame to ground level or even just a fraction above it, the Pickfords men having the luxury of all of three inches of clearance on this bridge. George Wooler is at the helm of the Manchester-based outfit supporting a 270-ton Parsons Peebles transformer destined for the Longannet power station in Fife.*

found that this airy type of trailer was ideally suited to carry their boilers as the load would sit securely in the frame itself. Straight girders, supported on bogies at either end were used in 1935 by E. W. Rudds to support the world's largest transformer at the time in Walton-on-Thames, but the same haulier discovered that if the girders were cranked at either end to form a crude swan-neck shape, then this lower-slung frame could support castings, stators and boilers as well as transformers at a far more manageable height.

Cranes of Dereham, Norfolk added a manufacturer's polish to the concept, producing Pickford's T3440 in the late 1940s. The sixteen solid-rubber wheels were able to support a payload of 140 tons, but the main attraction of 'the abortion' as the trailer was lovingly referred to, was the ability to vary the height of the girders through a system of four hydraulic rams. This tried principle had been used in part with the first Scammell 100 tonners so now not only could the trailer be lifted marginally to surmount road obstructions, it could also be lowered to creep under restrictive bridges. This was a big help but the greatest advantage of the variable suspension was to be that loading and especially unloading was now a far simpler procedure.

Static craneage in factories had kept pace with the increasing weight of their products but once away from their vicinity then only the docks had the mechanical means to lift the super weight as mobile craneage less than thirty years ago was extremely limited. The coming of the specialists like Sparrows and J. D. Whites was a long way off and heavy hauliers followed the example of Pickfords, Wynns and Millers who seemed to have the market to themselves with their lorry-based lifting mechanisms although the cranes had to work in tandem if more than 15 or 20 tons had to be picked up.

The design of the Crane girder trailers of the 1950s and '60s accelerated dramatically culminating in examples like Pickfords' TM1120 and TM1277, 300-ton capacity units on 48 massive pneumatic tyres. Wynns also had similar twelve-axle trailers although the strongest version bought by Sunters was SB1, again a Crane but only on six axles yet offering a capacity of 150 tons. In 1957 Sunters had bought SB3, an eight-axle, 90-ton capacity Crane unit which was originally destined for export but this one was a bit special in several senses of the word.

Fitted with two bogies of sixteen wheels each, they were mounted as four axles with four wheels in line. Relatively small tyres were used, 10.50 × 13 14 ply, which were not averse to blowing off, but their configuration was that the second and third axles in each bogie ran on a wider track to the steering first and fourth axles. This idea

Top *A slight variation in the frame type of trailer was Sunter's SB6 which offered a carrying capacity of 70 tons, its unladen weight being 28 tons. The carrying body was assembled to suit the load as the side girders, each about 14-ft long, could be lip joined together with a maximum of three per side. The Rolls Royce-powered Scammell is about to leave Workington with the Scheuerle in its fully extended form about 1963.*

Above *Modern-day girder trailers still come in a variety of shapes and capacities. Wrekin Roadways operated this 110-ton capacity Crane unit which also allowed independent use of the three-axled bogies for longer load work. The 150-ton capacity Scammell is hauling 93 tons of Brush electrical equipment from Lough-borough to Gladstone Dock, Liverpool during 1971.*

was all to do with spreading the weight and increasing the manoeuvr-ability of the trailer which was where the problems arose. The rear bogie steered automatically, the movement being sensed through the turning of the girders on the top-mounted bolster. This was the theory but in practice the rear bogie seemed to have sensors all of its own and when it felt like turning it just turned. The drivers spent more time looking in the mirror watching the rear end than they did looking forward, such was their concern for its unpredictability. Repeated visits back to Crane didn't solve the problem for many years and it caused one driver to pack in his job altogether. Travelling on a perfectly straight stretch of the A1 near Doncaster one day the empty trailer just shot off into the dyke because it felt like it. Close to a nervous breakdown over worrying about the trailer, the driver resigned, vowing no more.

Even with a tractor pushing there was no guarantee that the trailer would behave itself. The pusher driver did have a choice in the type of drawbar to use although most seemed to prefer to use a straight one. With an A bar you could take your hands off the wheel and read a newspaper if you wanted but it also meant that if the trailer shot off sideways then it dragged the tractor with it. The manufacturers insisted that the only thing wrong with this particular outfit was the fast speed it was driven at, but when running empty it took a great deal of resolve from the driver to keep the pace down to less than 20 mph.

The total independence of the modern-day girder trailer from out-side craneage is not an attribute which is won lightly, for its outward appearance doesn't suggest such an adaptable vehicle. To under-stand how this type of trailer unloads a massive transformer, one has to realize that the main frame girders are simply joined to the bogie/ necks by locating pins, albeit four rather large ones. Lowering the hydraulic suspension on either bogie will first drop the load on to suitable packing and further lowering will take all the weight off the girders. They will come to rest on two large roller skates which have been strategically placed on either side of the trailer close to one of its ends. Resting on the skates will allow two of the locating pins to be removed which will then separate one bogie/neck from the rest of the trailer. This bogie can now be pulled away from the load as can the other two thirds of the outfit, the massive girders, looking like two big arms, being trailed rather gingerly behind. Pushing these two parts together again will allow the trailer to be reformed, minus its load, ready for the unladen run back to base. Picking up a load of this nature is just the reverse of the unloading procedure but when you realize that Wynns' new girder trailers weigh in at around the 120-ton mark when empty, then it has to be appreciated that although the procedure may sound simple, in practice it takes quite a lot longer to perform.

It is the girders which are probably the biggest limiting factor for the longer they are made, the less load the outfit will be capable of carrying. They don't normally exceed more than 30 or 35 ft although to accommodate a large package boiler, Pickfords had some special extensions built and were able to carry a 48-ft 6-in-long load on TM1277. These side girders can be fitted at various heights on the bogie/necks, the loading points on the cargo dictating where they will be hung.

The girder trailer just oozes with an air of strength and reliability but being asked to support 200 or 300 tons can stretch that air just a little. 13 April 1966 was an unlucky day for Sunter driver Jock Fraser when he was hauling a 150-ton transmission auto transformer destined for Mannington in Hampshire. Routed the wrong way round a roundabout on the outskirts of Edinburgh, Jock found that the vicious adverse camber distorted a supporting beam so much that it gave way without warning, dropping the load on to the roadway. The outfit stopped. In fact it stopped so quickly that the mate being carried on top of the load to lift up telephone wires was catapulted off and suffered great physical discomfort when he came to a halt on reaching the ground. That the Northallerton staff coped with such an emergency is to their credit, with the load being delivered on time and undamaged. Subsequent forensic investigation into the fractured beam showed that a weld had given way due to an extreme drop in temperature the previous night. This is one reason why if a girder trailer is parked up loaded overnight, then the crew will lower the load off on to packing just to ease the weight fractionally off the hard-worked girders.

In SB6 Sunters were to operate quite a novel type of frame trailer. This was built by Scheuerle and had a carrying capacity of 70 tons with an unladen weight of 28 tons. It only had two sets of four wheels in line for each bogie but the frame consisted of six separate girders each approximately 14 ft long. Depending on the size of the load to be carried the trailer was built up using either two, four or all six short girders to make up the two sides with multi-use being possible as the side girders just lip joined to the next one or to the front and rear multi-wheeled bogies.

Automatic steering of the rear bogie, which made it turn in the opposite direction to the front one, was accomplished by running wires between the bogies at diagonals underneath the bottom of the trailer. Naturally these wires tended to stretch so they were later replaced by rods. These rods had to be made up in sections, to allow for variation in trailer length, but the joining knuckles tended to foul the cross supports on the load carrier rather than go smoothly through the holes that were made for them. To manoeuvre this rear

Above *Kingsnorth Fisher is one of the two specially-built ro-ro ships run by James Fisher of Barrow in Furness in conjunction with the CEGB. She is seen un-loading one of four Babcock & Wilcox pressure vessels weighing 277 tons that were destined for the BP refinery at Grangemouth. With load lengths varying between 65 ft and 77 ft carried in end suspension, Babcock's had constructed a special unloading ramp on the quayside to ease the incline back on to dry land.*

Below *Reflecting on the ingenuity of heavy haulage, this Wynn's outfit is re-ceiving a 140-ton vessel from the Maryke Irene which has been deliberately beached in Gelliswick Bay, Milford Haven. The 140-ft long, 16-ft diameter load was for delivery into the then new Amoco refinery built by Procon GB Ltd.*

bogie in a confined place the automatic rods were disconnected and a big bar was placed into the steering mechanism. Physical pressure on this bar caused the bogie to move in the desired direction but as many of the old Sunter crew will tell you, it was really hard work to move the heavily loaded bogie just fractionally.

In the 1960s the girder trailers saw their operations change slightly with two developments which had been promoted by the Central Electricity Generating Board. The least publicized of these two on the face of it had nothing to do with heavy haulage for they were in fact ships. They weren't the only two roll-on/roll-off ships in existence but *Aberthaw Fisher* and *Kingsnorth Fisher* have probably seen more girder trailer loads since they began operating in 1967 than all the other ro-ro ships put together. As can be guessed they are operated in conjunction with the Engineering Services Department of the CEGB by James Fisher and Sons Ltd of Barrow in Furness.

Delivering this 243-ton Ferranti generating transformer to the Foyers generating station on Loch Ness during September 1973 prompted the use of a variety of techniques. Carried by road to Pomona Dock, Manchester, the 30-ft long load was off loaded on to the Kingsnorth Fisher *who carried it to the Nigg Bay oil platform construction site. Here a 300-ton crane transhipped the mass on to a specially-set-up barge on which the carrying height had been amended to make it compatible to the unloading point. Bob Whitelaw is seen to be supervising the operation here, with both the unloading and the eventual move around the building perimeter being done by Scammell-based winching as there was no room for a cumbersome girder trailer on the small site.*

Close to being identical, *Aberthaw Fisher* was built in the Ailsa yard at Troon whilst *Kingsnorth Fisher* was launched from the Hall Russell yard at Aberdeen. The rather strange names come from the respective power stations that were to receive their maiden loads. At 1,500 tons, capable of 11 kt and fitted with twin screws plus a transverse thrust propeller fitted forward to give greater manoeuvrability, the greatest boon of these two ships is their shallow draught of only 12 ft. This gives them the ability to navigate inland waterways and river estuaries thus getting far closer to their destination power stations, as currently sixty ro-ro berths are being utilized in the United Kingdom and Northern Europe.

The method of loading is particularly interesting as the boats are fitted with an elevating and tilting platform, called the roadway, which adjusts to give a continuous gradient when lined up to the shore ramp or link span. Heavy girder trailers are normally pulled on board by winch as it can give far more control than a pushing tractor. Once on board the roadway is levelled out as the girder trailer stops with its load centred above the ship's lift. The girder trailer is split which allows the cargo to be lowered into the hold where a system of rails permits further winching off the lift. This is returned to deck level, the girder trailer hitches together again and the ship is ready to accept more cargo up to its capacity of 915 tons. The claim to having put the heaviest load on to one of the 'Fisher' boats does not come from Pickfords nor Wynns but from Chris Millers of Preston. On 11 May 1979, on one of their many runs to Dinorwic, Millers put ten assorted items on board weighing a total of 734 tons.

When compared to the 'Dock Express' ships of Rotterdam or even the 'Happy' fleet operated by Mammoet, then these two ships might not seem very large but their impact on modern heavy haulage in the United Kingdom is still very significant, which is perhaps not quite the case with the second CEGB development of 1967.

Although girder trailers had trebled their number of axles since the first pneumatic-tyred version in 1951, when you are carrying a 307-ton stator core it still means that each line of axles is supporting approximately 34 tons which is heavy for a newly strengthened bridge, never mind an old decaying one. With the introduction of air cushion equipment, the weight didn't disappear but it was spread more evenly down the entire length of the trailer and the critical axle loadings came down to about 22 tons a line.

Developed first by Vickers Ltd and then by the British Hovercraft Corporation, the system was based round a Commer Maxiload 16-tonner. Hidden underneath the soundproofed van bodywork built by Locomotors of Andover were four Rolls-Royce B51SV petrol engines each developing 235 bhp at 4,000 rpm. In practice they were utilized to produce compressed air via centrifugal blowers and could work up to 5½ psi, translated into weight support this meant 155 tons could be borne on the mass of air underneath the trailer itself. Getting it from the back of the Commer to the underneath of the girder outfit was achieved by reinforced ducting while to hold the pressure once it got there was made possible by first having the empty bottom of the trailer timbered out to form a temporary ceiling to the air. The membrane of the theoretical air box was made of neoprene rubber, the skirt part being reinforced with steel shoes on its base to allow it to slide over the roadway. Once blowing was completed, the skirt could be hitched up out of the way so it didn't affect the normal running of the road train too much. It was adaptable to any girder outfit, with minor modifications and thus wasn't restricted to one trailer or to one haulier.

ACE 1 was a tremendous success in doing what it set out to do and paid for itself over and over again in the amount of rebuilding costs it saved, but it wasn't perfect. Rigging and derigging of the trailer took a considerable amount of time and manpower expense. Preparing to blow and blowing was also very time consuming and although the system was replaced by ACE 2, which was more self-contained and efficient, Wynns Heavy Haulage, one of the greatest users of the equipment, started to rethink their strategy. Their answer was to simply stretch the girder trailer's length and add more axles to it. Thus on paper a 300-ton load, supported on a 120-ton trailer would still only run at 21 tons a line if twenty rows of axles were utilized. The outfit was certainly more unwieldy when going down the road but the modular axles brought new life to this singular trailer as well as being an ideal concept for supporting loads which had to be carried on more than one trailer.

Through the passage of time the heavy haulage business has seen virtually anything with wheels on pressed into use as a load-supporting bogie. Manufacturers like Cranes produced some very strong solid-tyred bogies but their use was not totally incident free. Jimmy Goulding was pulling a particularly heavy load one day with his Diamond T using a pair of these bogies to support the weight. With an almighty bang one of the solid tyres blew off, the remnants going underneath the tractor and into sight of the disconsolate driver. Pulling into the next suitable stopping place to assess his predicament Jimmy was pleased he had done so for as the solid lump of rubber had passed underneath the T it had sheared off the radiator

Above *The tank transporter, even in standard beaver-tail form was favoured by many hauliers as a general utility load carrier. Siddle Cook operated several units, their Gardner 6LW-engined Mountaineer being seen here in Park Lane, Gateshead after just leaving the works of Armstrong Whitworth in 1961. There are 31 tons in the roll on the transporter's back which is destined for export to the Algona Steel Corporation in Ontario.*

Opposite top *The type of bogies that can be used in heavy haulage vary tremendously. Wrekin Roadways are putting on show some of their assorted equipment in 1968 as they haul these 40-ton, 85-ft long crane girders through Leicestershire into BSC Corby. The second bogie was in fact a pneumatic conversion by Wrekin, the trailer originally starting life with Pickfords on solid tyres. David James also bought the following Scammell OEE 5, a 4 × 4 Mountaineer, second-hand but it was almost in mint condition having done very little work for its first owner, a farmer from Lincolnshire.*

Opposite middle *The Crane solid-tyred bogies may not have been very sophisticated but they were certainly strong. Sunter Bros worked their set very hard and regularly shared more than 200 tons of payload between them. There was only 95 tons in this Ashmore vessel which driver John Robinson is close to delivering as he makes the right turn towards Seal Sands in late 1967. Automatic steering of the back bogie is achieved by simply attaching the trailer drawbar to the overhead load.*

Opposite bottom *Taking up more than their fair share of roadway, Hill of Botley moved these two massive towers from the Terminus station at Southampton to Esso's oil refinery at Fawley during June 1970. With only a nominal width and weight of 53 tons and 39 tons respectively they did not overburden the Rolls-Royce engine of SPT 600 and PUC 474, the two hauling Constructors. Drivers Bill Miles and George Holbrook could only manage 4 mph for the seven-hour journey due to the column lengths of 132 ft and 147 ft. Naturally the Hill family were out in force, Chris Hill being the rear steersman on the leading load.*

drain tap and with all the coolant disappearing fast the Cummins would have seized up solid had not Jimmy stopped in time.

These bogies were immensely strong, although as Peter Sunter would tell their suspension was rather limited. He was shepherding

Above *These particular transporters known as SMTs were modified by Hill of Botley to make practicable use of them as bogies. 298 FUW started life with the Royal Navy and was converted to ballasted-tractor form by Hill. The outfit is seen in 1962 about to leave Marchwood railway station with an 85-ft long 60-ton girder for Fawley power station.*

Below *The Scheuerle hydraulically-suspended trailer introduced an entirely new concept to the heavy haulage world. Useable as either two separate four-axle bogies or, as Strathclyde are using it, in eight-axle form, the load carrier offered both variable suspension and automatic steering. There is not a lot of weight in this fermenting tank hauled from Kent to Edinburgh for Scottish and Newcastle Breweries, but the Scheuerle did offer a capacity of 150 tons in its fully-loaded state.*

Above *Built as a reply to the German version, Cranes of Norfolk produced for Pickfords this set of bogies numbered TM870/A and B. Having a slightly higher running height than the German trailer, the Crane bogies were also much stronger having a capacity of 200 tons in eight-axle form. George Revell and Jack Richards are the two Sheffield-based Pickfords men seen on Babcock's premises checking the 165-ton steam drum.*

Below *Also built specially for Pickfords were TM1518 and TM1519, two six-axle bogies manufactured by King. Their hydraulic suspension was utilized to self load these 174-ton oil loading buoys in September 1973 after they had been assembled at King George V Dock, Glasgow. At 48 ft diameter and 40 ft high, the loads were moved round the dock by Contractor M4965 to within lifting range of Magnus II, the floating crane.*

one of their long loads one day on the prescribed route between Stockton and Middlesbrough which includes the surmounting of Leven Bank. At one in seven gradient the bank is not one of the steepest but a severe turn a third of the way up certainly adds spice to the climb with a lengthy vessel. This particular load made the bogies creak and groan as the weight began to count and although the wheels tried their best to follow the twisting camber, Peter reported one of the little tyres was a good foot off the ground as the turn was made.

Rather than pay the manufacturer's price however for this proven product, lots of hauliers pressed old War Department trailers into use for a fraction of the cost with tank transporters being one of the most favoured purchases. These trailers weren't in the main very long but they were found to be very adaptable in that they could be used singly for loads of concentrated weight or in pairs to act as long-length bogies. Sixteen, 24 or even 32 pneumatic tyres were used teamed together in twins but this was sometimes a blessing in disguise.

Peter Clemmett was driving an Elliotts of York outfit using a newly acquired tank transporter to carry his heavy cargo which was collected from the heart of London. Unfortunately, having stood in a field

The Nicolas modular trailer proved popular with many operators. Pickfords are seen to be using twelve rows with this Babcock load in 1984 not only because of the weight, which was only 90 tons, but because at 84 ft long and 27 ft wide, the load demanded great stability. It was in fact the centre section of a coal unloading boom being built at Castle Peak, Hong Kong.

The fourteen rows of Nicolas used by Econofreight to move this Lamberton roller straightener locally on Teesside during early 1985 were certainly taxed, for the 20-ft wide load weighed in at an impressive 294 tons. The haulier undertook the tricky in-site removal utilizing self-climbing jacks to lift the machine 11 ft into the air. The steering attributes of the Nicolas are well demonstrated with an all-up weight close to 400 tons.

unused and unwanted for years on end had not done the tyres of the trailer any good and once they were asked to support a substantial weight they naturally rebelled. Peter recalls that it took him a week to get through the metropolis with the night-time escorts being of a very short nature as progress was continually interrupted by tyres bursting open. Peter's days were spent putting new tyres on and anyone who has attempted to change these awkward inner wheels will know what a swine of a job it can be.

When Wynns bought their new flat top from Scheuerle in 1957 trailers were set for a dramatic change, for in essence this eight-axle trailer was made to divide into two separate four-axle bogies. A similar join-up principle was adopted in a set of Crane bogies also bought by Wynns, the twelve rows of axles comprising two sets of four rows plus two of two rows. Pickfords also operated similar Crane bogies and King produced their TM1518 and TM1519, two six-axle units that could be linked together both fore and aft or even made to run side by side. In the main however these were rather special trailers built to order and it wasn't until the early 1970s that the products of Nicolas from France and Commetto of Italy arrived in the United Kingdom. These new axles were the start of the modular trailer boom which was

Above *One way round excessive overloads of the tractor-drive axle was to use a jeep dolly. Close examination of this early Scania of British Ropes will reveal the tractor is a four-wheeler coupled to a jeep dolly, thus giving the appearance of a six-wheeled unit. This type of outfit was favoured in the late 1960s although it was actually illegal as the law said that a heavy motor car could not haul two trailers unless specifically authorized.*

Top left *These six-axle Goldhoffer semi-trailers used by Sunters were well liked, especially for Continental work as the hydraulically-suspended self-steering units were able to comply with the tight turning circle limits imposed upon them. However, as the trailer was extended the axles obviously go further back, thus creating the problem of more weight to be taken through the tractor king pin. There is 58 tons in these 11-ft 6-in wide Davy vessels about to leave Teesside and destined for Yugoslavia.*

Middle left *The modular trailer concept was soon utilized to produce a semi-trailer that could have its neck, bed and running gear bolted together to suit whatever job it had to do. The Dow Mac photograph shows Watkinson's Scania OWX 595M coupled to a Cometto version carrying a 75-ton lump destined for Butterwick near Scunthorpe in October 1977.*

Bottom left *Wrekin Roadways also got good service from Cometto modular gear. Here their four-axle semi-trailer is supporting 93 tons in the guise of the Great Western Railway's No 6000 King George V. The photograph shows the outfit, driven by Cyril Potter, in 1978 at Ross on Wye en route from the Bulmer Railway Centre at Hereford to British Rail Engineering at Swindon. The Cummins 350-powered Foden 100-tonner was taking its stronger counterpart for an overhaul prior to a special Paddington-to-Swindon run under steam.*

to totally revolutionize heavy haulage, not only in the way the haulier could assemble his own trailer to suit the job in hand but also in the type of load that he was now capable of hauling.

Sunters ably demonstrated the concept of building trailers for loads when they moved that 221 ft column in March 1984. Although visually it just seemed as though they were using one bogie with eight rows of axles and a second bogie with ten rows, the leading bogie did in fact comprise two four-row bogies joined together end to end although the other bogie consisted of four separate trailers all assembled together. Two five-row bogies were linked to produce ten rows of axles but alongside were two half-width trailers giving the bogie twelve small tyres in each row of axles, a configuration which is termed as three-file wide.

Don't think, however, that assembling the new modular equipment is just like building up Meccano, it is hard and it is meticulous. The high pressure hydraulic hosing has to be piped in and bled free of air, but it is the different track rods which affect the steering geometry that are the most laborious to set up.

As well as forming independent bogies the modular axles can be built up to form one long single trailer, one of the biggest examples seen on road work being of 24 axles in length. They were used to carry the Davy castings when they were trundled down the M18/M1 between Doncaster and Sheffield. A breath of fresh air was also given to the semi-trailer using the modular idea with the swan neck, trailer bed and multi rows of axles being interchangeable to suit the job. This

In foreign climes the two-trailer concept was openly used as an obvious way not to overload the hauling tractor. The two distinct trailers are more obvious in this shot taken on 2 February 1964 as the well-turned-out Super Hippo is about to receive the C. A. Parsons stator in Trinidad, West Indies.

increased the scope of the heavyweight artic in a legal manner which was unlike the attempt first made in the late 1960s to increase their capability.

The jeep dolly looks a fairly innocuous piece of equipment but as far as the law is concerned it is a trailer. What some hauliers were doing was to hook up a jeep dolly to their tractive unit, which at a brief glance made a four-wheeler appear to be a six-wheeler, before hitching up the load-carrying semi-trailer. This practice took weight from the tractive unit drive axle and gave the haulier a far more adaptable vehicle, but the law enforcers simply said this was using a heavy motor car to draw two trailers which, even under the Special Types General Order, was not allowed. That is not to say that there are no jeep dolly outfits being used on the road, but each of these modern-day versions are specifically authorized after strict vetting by the Department of Transport who are very conscious of the difficulty in reversing the double articulating outfit and its susceptibility to jack knifing.

Dowsett Engineering are one company who speak very highly of the jeep dolly as they have, for quite some time, operated a DAF 3300 6 × 4 unit which coupled to a variable Nooteboom semi-trailer. For grossing no more than 50 or 55 tons, the low loader was simply a two-axled version. However as the payload increased or the need to reduce individual axle loads became greater, Dowsetts simply added a jeep dolly to the tractive unit and/or another pair of axles to the end of the semi-trailer which converted the five-axle outfit into one with either six, seven or eight axles.

For those operators who don't want or can't get a specially authorized jeep dolly outfit there is an alternative which is also capable of heavyweight use yet still does not overtax the drive axles. Nicolas of France were to offer an early version which saw a pair of steerable axles mounted on the semi-trailer immediately behind the swan neck. Craven Tasker produced a similar type for Cadzow Heavy Haulage although it was the version produced by King that found greater acceptance amongst the heavy-plant-hauling fraternity. The Market Harborough 90-ton capacity version looks very much like a single-axle jeep dolly addition but to ensure legality this axle is a permanent attachment to the semi-trailer.

King have produced quite a variety of configurations of modular semi-trailers, but perhaps the TS100/7ES operated by Redhouse Garage Company of Coventry is the most unusual. The package bought by Redhouse comprised two trombone step-frame semi-trailers, one with three axles and the other with four, their variable

Above *A legal way round non-jeep dolly use is shown in this Nicolas semi-trailer used by Sunters of Northallerton where a pair of axles fitted right at the front of the load carrier ensures the tractor does not take an excess part of the weight. B950 ACA was a demonstrator put out by Fodens and rated at a 150 tons gross operation. It had a 400 Cummins engine and a twenty-speed Spicer gearbox but a rather high Kenworth rear bogie.*

Below *As the unending capabilities of the modular trailer became realized then the loads they were asked to carry just grew and grew. This skittle-like construction was one of three similar loads built by Babcock & Wilcox which Pickfords hauled to Glasgow docks prior to export to Russia in 1976. At 30-ft high and 218 tons in weight it demanded delicate carriage, with only plus or minus two degrees out of horizontal permitted. Driver Andy Higgins was only required to keep a ½ mph average speed and Pickfords' manager John Banks described it as the most sensitive job that he he had ever done.*

It was in the booming oil construction centres that the multi-wheeled modular trailer really came to the fore, hauling constructions that were to take the breath away due to their sheer size. This BP photograph taken at Sullom Voe on 11 August 1978 shows the arrival of the first PAU (pre-assembled unit) on site, it having been built by Burntisland Fabrication and Engineering Ltd. At approximately 40 ft in each direction, the unit weighed 338 tons so Rigging International decided to utilize one of their Lampson crawlers to head their well-travelled 4 × 4 Hough.

length being between 40 and 59 ft. However if a capacity of 102 tons is required the axles from one semi-trailer are simply removed and clipped on to the back of the other semi-trailer giving a version with seven axles, although in this form the trailer must remain unextended. To ensure manoeuvrability in this new generation of semi-trailers, sensors are fitted near the king pin which activate automatic steering by means of hydraulics on most of these rear axles.

The modular trailer concept may have brought a new way of thought to the semi-trailer but it totally revolutionized what the heavy haulier was able to move in the fast-developing oil rig yards. Loading modules of over 3,000 tons in weight on to sea-going barges was not a regular occurrence, but loads of 2,000 tons were quite common. The modular trailer gave smooth support to constructions of 200 ft in height, the inbuilt jacking system of the suspension being ideal to lift the load off or place it down on to the loading plinths or stools. However, time stands still for no one and development in this particular field took a dramatic leap forward, its results first being seen in the United Kingdom during 1985.

This page *Just as the modular trailer breathed new life into heavy haulage operations, the arrival of the self-propelled trailer seems set to oust it from the load-out business. Mammoet's Scheuerle units show off their manoeuvrability. One of the many pluses of this equipment is that it is controlled solely by one man.*

Self-propelled trailers weren't a new idea, for the German company of Scheuerle had first developed them into use during 1975. As the name implies they carry their own engine, so unlike the modular trailers they don't require a pulling tractor or a winch to make them move. The price tag of the ones in use by Mammoet of Holland may be twice the price of similar-sized conventional modular axles but their assets of performance are far more than twice as good. Linking the new units together is completed in minutes rather than hours; no matter how many separate trailers are put under a load their movement is controlled by one man only with a simple console, carried by a neck strap, not by an assortment of tractor drivers or winch operators, but the biggest plus of the SPT is its sheer manoeuvrability. The modular trailer tends to run in straight lines, backwards or forwards, with the steering being fairly slow to take effect. In contrast the hydrostatic propulsion of individual axles on the SPT means it can go forwards, backwards, sideways or even be made to rotate about its own centre if you want, a sophisticated, easy-to-operate computer taking all the guesswork out of programming.

The arrival of the SPT is bound to affect the United Kingdom heavy haulage industry for as Mammoet have demonstrated, they can move a module in Hartlepool, the units can be unclipped, placed on the back of road-going 40-ft semi-trailers and be shipped back to Holland on the overnight ferry to move a load out there the next day.

At long last the development of equipment seems to have caught up with the demands placed on the heavy haulier although there will always be the occasional load that needs flair and imagination to deliver it. Such a move was involved in the shipment and installation of a 1,300-ton pressurized water reactor from Vickers in Barrow, to Dounreay in Scotland during June 1985. The sea part of the haul was done in a fairly conventional manner with the reactor being carried on a small barge which in turn was floated on to *Giant 2* another huge semi-submersible load carrier which in turn was hauled by an 11,500-hp tug. The 380 miles by sea was straightforward but it was the headache of the last mile on dry land to get the reactor close to its final resting point which required quite an interesting technique to be adopted.

Once the load-carrying barge had been beached on to dry land, winches, which were mounted at the front of the barge, operated via a system of dead man points positioned alongside the temporary roadway so that it was able to drag itself along. But at close to 3,000 tons all-up weight, friction across the sandy surface had to be eased and to do this the barge was rolled over a series of 25-ft long, 30-in

The first demonstration in the United Kingdom of the capabilities of the SPTs was seen in Hartlepool in March 1985 when Mammoet loaded out from the premises of MM Oil this 160-ft high, 780-ton jacket frame destined for the North Sea. The umbilical type wires running between the four separate SPTs ensures complete co-ordination although the most noticeable thing about the photograph is the lack of winch ropes and heavy locomotives.

diameter rubber air bags which were squeezed almost flat as the weight passed over them. The mile-long journey may have taken five days to complete but it was quicker and cheaper than building a very expensive super strength conventional roadway to take this one-off load.

With the demonstration of this type of technique there seems to be no limit to the mountains which can be moved by the enterprising heavy haulier.

Index